AMERICAN INDIAN ARTIFACTS

AMERICAN INDIAN ARTIFACTS
HOW TO IDENTIFY, EVALUATE AND CARE FOR YOUR COLLECTION

BY ELLEN WOODS

SEVEN LOCKS PRESS
Santa Ana, California
Minneapolis, Minnesota
Washington, D.C.

Library of Congress Cataloging in Publication Data

Woods, Ellen, 1948–
    American Indian Artifacts: How to Identify, Evaluate and Care for Your Collection
        p.   cm.
    Includes bibliographical references.
    ISBN 0-929765-55-9
    1. Indians of North America--Material culture.   2. Indians of North America--
Antiquities--Collectors and collecting.   3. Indians of North America--Antiquities--
Collection and preservation.
    I. Title.

    E98.M34W66   1997
970'.00497'0075--dc21   96-54237
                                                                      CIP

Manufactured in the United States of America

SEVEN LOCKS PRESS
P.O. Box 25689
Santa Ana, CA 92799
(800) 354-5348

For the one who calls me Bruha

"My mom's earliest memories include searching for arrowheads in the Southern California desert with her father and two brothers. The time they spent together and the excitement of finding something so old and beautiful made those memories among the best of her life. American Indians and their art have fascinated my mother ever since. Teaching people about American Indian art, traditions, and customs has been something she has enjoyed doing for the past twenty years. I can honestly say she is one of a few people who are able to make a living doing something that she has always loved."

Mike Randazzo

CONTENTS

FOREWORD

The lure of the past manifests in the love and desire to have pieces of the ancient picture. The first peoples of the Americas found that persons from other cultures (whether non-Indian or other indigenous neighbors) were eager to collect parts of their everyday living experiences. Later to be known as American Indians, they made their implements of life and spirituality from nature itself, sometimes in combination with non-Indian trade items. Therefore, no two individually created and labor-intensive artifacts were exact copies of one another.

These indigenous people incorporated pride into the creation of everyday utility items so that they became art imbued with subtle sacred meanings. Sacred implements were also art. The act of living was never separated from art or sacredness, and no words existed that could separate the person from either. The beauty and specialness meant to be incorporated into life's very breath was shared by all. This positive and sophisticated attitude brought dignity and benefits to everyone involved with those necessary tools.

These special attributes of American Indian artifacts have universal appeal. Collectors past and present are found globally. Intellectual curiosity always accompanies the joy of ownership. Being able to establish correctly the identity of an artifact requires having an open and inquiring mind. This is essential because often the zeal of adding to a collection will blind or coerce judgment to bend the truth about the artifact to fit the needs of the collector. The truth is possible if the seeker is able to travel nationwide immersed in the identification and cross-comparison of countless articles from the American Indian past. It is also necessary to have access to knowledgeable persons and to study valid accounts in order to acquire valuable insights and make intelligent formulations.

Numerous reference materials on the many subjects about the American Indians and their artifacts exist, however, to research a collectible, a collector must have many sources. *American Indian Artifacts* consolidates vast amounts of information into a handy and clearly written small reference text that covers history, identification, and laws. The recognized American Indian cultural sensitivity and attention to detail evident within these pages reflect Ellen Woods' Sioux, Cree, and Delaware heritages and are offered in loving honor of all native peoples' ancestors.

This book contains expert knowledge gleaned from years of extensive research. The author's travels constantly crisscross the North American continent and always includes in-depth studying plus collecting at museums, shows, and fellow collectors' homes. Ms. Woods is recognized nationwide as an appraiser, researcher, and buyer of American Indian artifacts and art. Her prominence in this highly specialized field has led to many alliances with colleges, universities, and museums including the television and movie industries as a consultant.

This book is not only enjoyable to read but is an invaluable sourcebook for persons interested in and a must for all collectors of North American Indian artifacts.

Gloria Bodgon, Cherokee
Professor of Anthropology

Orange Coast College
Costa Mesa, California

ACKNOWLEDGMENTS

This book is an acknowledgment of all those who had faith in me, who believed I could do whatever I set my mind to.

Many thanks to Gloria and Tom Bodgon for their support during the past few years and for their help in urging me forward.

Thanks also to Denise Estrella for all the time given in editing and typing; Patti Gantes for the great work on the diagrams and maps; Matt Richey for the time he took to photograph the many artifacts pictured in this book; and to David and Penny Schneiderman because they were there.

A very special acknowledgment to Fred Wayne Popejoy who got me started collecting when I was a small girl; and to Mike Randazzo, my son, who gave me help on the computer.

And last but not least, my daughter and her family, Elizabeth, Manuel, and Todd Hidalgo; they know why.

Tlingit basket, southeastern Alaska

1

COLLECTING AMERICAN INDIAN ART AND ARTIFACTS

Collecting is fun! That is why people are collectors. But there are even more good reasons for collecting American Indian artifacts. There is the satisfaction of gathering history where it can be viewed, touched, and studied, but there is still another reason: each and every American Indian piece has been crafted by a person putting his or her spirit and soul into that object.

Part of the fun of collecting American Indian artifacts comes from possession of the objects after the excitement of hunting them down. Rarity, uniqueness, and beautiful attention to detail of these collectibles lure us into craving more and more of these pieces.

There is the old saying that "a piece can speak to you." This may be even more true about American Indian art. Most collectors of American Indian art and artifacts are nearly spellbound with enthusiasm over their hobby. Most collect for the enjoyment it gives them, but they also like the investment, especially since the market for these collectibles has been strongly advancing for many years. Of course, there are some folks who buy and hold American Indian items for the investment only, but they are few and are considered investors rather than collectors. So the enjoyment of collecting American Indian art and artifacts ultimately comes from the ownership of historical items made by people who were spiritually and physically in harmony with their surroundings when the objects were made, thereby transforming an energy to the art form.

Map 1. Culture areas of North American Indians

American Indians made their crafts and utilitarian pieces in a traditional manner with their tribe or group, yet they put their individual creativity into each piece. That is why every piece is unique while retaining a certain similarity to work of the artist's tribe.

The first collectors of American Indian artifacts were the American Indians themselves. Archaeological studies show that distant tribes met with each other and traded their fine prehistoric jewelry, pieces of stone, trade metals, beads, and various utilitarian items. True, some pieces were traded out of necessity, but it is believed that many were collected for their beauty, rarity, importance, and desirability.

When the European explorers first arrived, they seized the opportunity to take native objects home with them. In fact, some of the finest collections of American Indian art are in Europe.

Many famous people have collected American Indian art. Wild Bill Cody, William Randolph Hearst, and Senator Barry Goldwater are just a few collectors who spent at least part of their lives searching out American Indian objects. Presently, Robert Redford, Barbra Streisand, Whoopi Goldberg, Linda Ronstadt, and George Lucas are a few of the many well-known people who also enjoy collecting American Indian art.

Museums throughout the United States and in many foreign countries have great collections of American Indian art. I have prepared a short list to aid you in enjoying and studying at these museums (chapter 9). You will find many more in your travels. Before visiting a museum, call ahead for the times that they are open, as most have restricted hours. Also, if you are planning on doing research call ahead to get permission to study pieces that are not out on display. Display room is very limited at museums, and most holdings are kept in storage. Do not be bashful; museum people are there to help you.

TYPES OF COLLECTIONS

Unlike myself, most people are not general collectors of American Indian art. There are many categories of items to collect, so most people specialize in one or more areas.

In breaking down these areas, I first considered the groups and then the types of items under each group. The groups from which to collect are:

Baskets	Weavings
Pottery	Jewelry
Quillwork and beadwork	Stone, bone, horn, shell,
Wood and hide pieces	and ivory pieces

It is easy to find specialized areas of collecting in American Indian art and artifacts. There are some very large collections of specialized items, and they are just as much fun as general collections.

AVAILABILITY OF AMERICAN INDIAN COLLECTIBLES

A very important ingredient of any successful collection is availability. Unless collectibles are available to purchase, possess, and enjoy, one cannot accumulate a decent collection. Fortunately, in American Indian art there is everything from the very rare, hard-to-find items to the overly plentiful.

It is your choice to collect within the level of availability you prefer. For example, rare classic weavings are very limited in availability and the prices are high. If you are willing to pay the price, however, the availability is there. On the other hand, Navajo rugs of lesser quality are plentiful and not difficult to find.

Prehistoric pottery is plentiful because thousands of pottery pieces were made and thousands have been found. Prehistoric jewelry is exceptionally hard to find as more was made than has survived. Prehistoric stone items such as arrowheads are quite available and are still being found. Rare flint Paleo points are expensive and hard to acquire.

Certain historic (after there were written records) American Indian artifacts are very scarce. Examples are pre-reservation beadwork and quillwork, wooden pieces, and very early baskets. In contrast, quite available for collecting are reservation-period beadwork and early 1900s pottery, baskets, jewelry, and weavings.

American Indian jewelry provides the collector with an array of types and qualities. An additional attraction is that you can display some of your jewelry while you are wearing it.

So let's get collecting; the availability and good prices are out there!

WHERE TO FIND COLLECTIBLES

Early collectors could buy many items directly from the American Indians, and stone collectors could hunt for arrowheads on old American Indian camping sites. Today we have to hunt for collectibles at shows, antique stores, dealers, galleries, shops, auctions, flea markets, garage sales, and many other places.

There are special shows where you can view and purchase American Indian collectibles. At the end of this book you will find a list of the promoters of quality American Indian and ethnographic shows; you can contact them for dates and places. These shows consist of dealers, collectors, and American Indian artists displaying their wares for sale. American Indian shows are an excellent place to meet people who share your same interests, to purchase collectibles, to study collections, and to keep you on top of the market values. Antique shows and gun shows often have American Indian items displayed for sale.

Dealers trade American Indian art and artifacts on a regular basis. You will find dealers in every area and from all walks of life. A good place to meet them is at American Indian shows. Serious collectors usually keep in contact with at least two dealers in whom they trust and with whom they can work closely. The advantages of buying from a dealer are:

1. Reputable dealers stand behind their sales.
2. The product can be examined as closely as you wish.
3. Price, terms, and conditions can be negotiated.
4. Dealers share their experience and knowledge with you.
5. Dealers can locate hard-to-find pieces for you.

Another good place to find American Indian relics is in other collections. Most collectors are interested in trading or selling to upgrade their collections.

Galleries and American Indian stores across the country carry beautiful art work and artifacts. Simply look in the yellow pages under Galleries or Indian Goods.

Mail order is also available to collectors. Some dealers, galleries, and stores have catalogs and lists of American Indian items they wish to sell. One publication specializes in picturing American Indian items for sale. Dealers do a large amount of their business by sending photographs of items for sale.

During the last few years a trend of selling at auctions has developed. There are many large auction houses that hold special American Indian and ethnographic auctions once or twice a year. Smaller auction houses hold them more often.

Buying and selling at auctions is all right as long as you understand what you are doing. The good points are:

1. Large quantities of material are available in one location.
2. Some good art can be purchased there.
3. Markets are set there.

The disadvantages are:

1. You purchase *as is.* That means that what you saw or did not see is what you purchased. No guarantee is given as to authenticity, age, and condition. (People know this and often dump pieces that are not authentic at auctions.)
2. Some items are owned by the auctioneer.
3. You have to pay a buyer's premium at most auctions whether the auctioneer owns it or not.
4. Reserves and set minimums often do not let you in to buy until a near-market figure is reached.

The day of an estate-type sale where there is no minimum set price beforehand is pretty much over for American Indian items. Auctions are fun and I do recommend that you buy at them, as long as you understand the conditions. Most important is that you preview each item and get help if you are not sure about something because, as the auctioneer will tell you, once the gavel is down, you own it.

A fun place to hunt for American Indian items is at flea markets, garage sales, or just generally around your neighborhood. You will be surprised how many of your friends know of items. Flea markets and yard sales are loaded with replicas and poor-quality items, but you can occasionally find great pieces.

LEARNING ABOUT THE HOBBY

It is important for collectors to learn everything they can about American Indian art. This can be done by visiting museums, going to shows, visiting other collectors and their collections, reviewing videotapes, visiting research libraries, and reading every book possible on the subject.

I have discussed shows that display and sell Indian items. Be sure to visit as many as possible and ask questions of the exhibitors. Shows are a focal point at which collectors and dealers meet.

Find out where other collectors are and study their items. Other collectors do not often find people who share their interests and usually will enjoy burning the midnight oil with you.

More and more videotapes are coming out on American Indian art. Videos are very educational, reasonably priced, and fun to watch. There are videos on baskets, weavings, pottery, stone, and other collectibles.

Better yet, build your own library. Book dealers who specialize in American Indian books are usually at the Indian shows. There are excellent reference books available on each subject. Unfortunately, most American Indian books are very specialized, and looking anything up requires several different books.

A must for every collector is at least one of the periodicals published. There are not very many and I have listed a few of them for you at the end of the book. Show dates, exhibits, articles, and advertisements are all in these periodicals. You can open up the world of collecting by subscribing to one or more of them.

Other excellent sources of information are the colleges and universities that teach subjects relating to the American Indian. Check with your local institutions of higher learning to see what is being offered on this subject.

CARING FOR YOUR COLLECTION

In the chapters following I discuss specific groups of artifacts and explain in detail how to care for your collection.

Half the fun of owning a good collection is the enjoyment of showing it to others. Therefore, displaying your collection is very important. The cost of good display cabinets is very minor in comparison to the value of the items you will put into the cases. Yet, I have seen great pieces left unprotected because the collector did not want to spend money on display cases.

Most collections get too big to display everything at once, so storage is necessary. Read carefully about how to store your items.

Some American Indian collectibles such as baskets, weavings, wooden items, beadwork, and quillwork are susceptible to insect damage. There is nothing worse than finding a very valuable, nonreplaceable piece of art destroyed by insects. Too often, I have seen damage done by pets and small children. Good protection as described in this book should save great pieces.

Cleaning is also important to preserve the pieces and give them a neat appearance. There are some cleaning methods that can be used on a collection. Please refer to each chapter that pertains to your type of collectible for information on cleaning.

RECORD KEEPING

Most collections lack one thing: records of the collectibles. I recommend tagging or labeling each piece with an identification number that corresponds to the same pertinent information on a 3 x 5 card, in a ledger, or stored in a computer database file.

I also recommend a videotape of your entire collection, for not only can you enjoy it without handling the objects, but videotapes make an excellent record for insurance purposes. Keep a copy of the video in a safe-deposit box.

This brings up insurance. If it is possible, you should cover some of your collection under your homeowner's insurance policy. Most collections are so large, however, that they require separate coverage. The cost of coverage can become so expensive, however, it sometimes prohibits insuring the collection.

SHOULD YOUR COLLECTION BE APPRAISED?

Yes, because a collector who knows the retail market value of each of his or her collectibles is a better buyer, seller, and trader. Also, you will need an outsider's professional appraisal for insurance purposes or theft reports, even when simply shipping items to other people, as any loss must be documented with a value to properly collect the insurance.

Who should appraise your collection? Too often, outside appraisers do certified appraisals so far from actual market values that collectors have difficulty selling or collecting insurance. I have seen a collection appraised at $500,000, worth actually less than half that amount, while other times the opposite occurs. Knowing the everyday values of American Indian art and artifacts is hard, even for those in the business.

What is interesting is that the cost of an appraisal has not risen with the rest of the economy, so a whole collection can be appraised very reasonably. To locate a good appraiser in the business, contact anyone who buys and sells, or check the trade periodicals.

RESTORATION

Restoration may be more common in American Indian collectibles than collectors sometimes realize. Replacement of beads on beadwork, brightening of paint on pottery, and addition of new stitches on baskets are all fairly common occurrences today. However, most restoration can be detected and nonrestored pieces are available for collectors who want them.

If the collector has a piece in need of repair, there are professional restorers who advertise in the trade papers and attend most American Indian shows. When should you have restoration done? When it saves a piece from further deterioration and when it makes economic sense. If a basket retails at

$400 and repairing it would cost $300, it may not make good business sense to restore it, unless you paid less than $100 for it.

Restoration can change the value of an item in two ways: first, the full retail value of a repaired collection is less than one with no repairs; second, if it is a damaged great piece bought reasonably and the cost of repairs is small, the repaired piece may be much more valuable when finished. There is no exact percentage of difference established, but certainly there is a difference.

FAKES, REPRODUCTIONS, AND FACSIMILES

By any name, reproductions are not good items for your American Indian collection. People usually collect for the enjoyment of possessing, studying, and viewing authentic American Indian items that were crafted with the hands and spirit of American Indian artists. Any fake, reproduction, or facsimile would not have that same charm for you.

Unfortunately, any collectible that becomes valuable can be copied, and reproductions are sometimes represented as authentic. It is usually not the reproduction artists who put fakes into the authentic market; it is often the second or third party who, knowingly or not, put the piece on the market.

In what forms do reproductions or fakes occur?

1. Complete reproductions made from exact materials the American Indians used, then aged to look old
2. Conglomerates: many authentic pieces put together to make one authentic looking, marketable item
3. Replicas made to look like authentic artifacts but of materials different from those originally used

You should not give up on collecting if you buy or trade into a fake. We have all had that happen. Chalk it up to a learning experience. The enjoyment from collecting authentic American Indian art makes up at least tenfold for the few bad experiences you will have with reproductions. In each chapter I will discuss how to detect nonauthentic pieces.

Authentic reproductions are new American Indian-made pieces that are nearly exact copies of their ancestors' relics. There are companies and individual artists making Plains Indian items, jewelry, and other fine artwork. This work is a recognized art form and should not be confused with non-Indian reproductions.

Non-Indian replicas are sometimes sold at shows, galleries, stores, flea markets, and Mountain Man shows as replicas. There are no problems once the buyer is aware these pieces are not American Indian made, are nontraditional, and are mainly for decoration. Problems occur when collectors encounter non-Indian replicas that are being sold as authentic American Indian items.

Be careful when the description of any item is too vague or is loose, e.g., "Indian style," "Pueblo" (without a name), "handwoven" (without the tribe who wove it).

GOVERNMENT LAWS

Listed below are some laws that pertain to American Indian art collectibles. The early laws mainly affect prehistoric Indian items.

The Federal Antiquities Act (1906) prohibits damaging, excavating, and removal of related items from Indian sites on federal lands. This early law had little effect due to small fines and poor enforcement. Thus, the next law was enacted.

Public Law 96–95, The Archaeological Resources Protection Act of 1979, says that archaeological resources on public and American Indian lands are further protected by more severe penalties. No one is allowed to excavate, remove, damage, alter, or deface any archaeological resources on federal government lands. Also, no one can legally purchase, sell, trade, transport, receive, or offer for sale any archaeological resource taken illegally from federal land.

In addition, no one can sell, purchase, or exchange in interstate or foreign commerce any archaeological resources involved in violation of any local or state law. This final paragraph was recently used to prosecute a collector who collected on private land without written permission from the property owner.

Confusion about field collecting of arrowheads exists because some federal laws allow it, but many agencies within the federal government prohibit it. It is always best to check with your local and state governments and federal agencies about the laws. Before hunting on private land, obtain permission from the property owner, or the American Indian objects collected may be considered unlawfully obtained and fall under federal law when the pieces cross a state line.

Many states have enacted laws prohibiting the excavation of American Indian burial sites on privately owned land. Arizona passed such a law in 1990 and New Mexico has a similar law.

The following laws affect historical American Indian items:

> Feather Laws:
> Migratory Bird Treaty Act (1918)
> Bald Eagle Protection Act (1940 & 1962)
> Endangered Species Act (1973)
> Agency laws of Fish and Wildlife Services
> All state and local laws

Because eagle feathers were used on American Indian war bonnets, dance bustles, fans, and many other items, these laws directly affect the buying, selling, trading, and bartering of thousands of rare old American Indian relics. Unfortunately, the legislators did not grandfather in the old pieces, so they are also affected. Due to these laws, many feathered artifacts have been destroyed or damaged by removal of feathers.

It is unlawful in many states to buy, sell, or trade in game animal parts. In California, fish and game laws prohibit trading in almost all wild game animal parts, including bear parts. Federal law protects the grizzly bear and its parts.

A recently passed federal law that is influencing historical American Indian artifacts is the Native American Graves Protection and Repatriation Act of 1990 (NAGPRA). This law is clear about prohibiting the removal of human remains and grave goods from American Indian burials located on federal lands, and this applies to institutions receiving federal funds.

One section of this law is confusing and worries museums, collectors, and dealers because it discusses giving back sacred and cultural patrimonial type items to the Indian nations from which they originated. The interpretation that can be given to the terms used in the act is very broad.

There are two laws that impact contemporary American Indian art. Federal Public Law 191–644, Indian Art and Crafts Act of 1990, mainly covers the import of objects sold as American Indian made, when the pieces are actually made by other than American Indians. It also covers those that claim items are American Indian made when they are not. New Mexico's Indian Arts and Crafts Act of 1978 (amended in 1991) makes it unlawful to barter, sell, or trade any items represented as American Indian made unless they are produced or created by American Indians. New Mexico's law also requires that items for sale be tagged stating what material the items are made of, whether machine or handmade, and whether natural materials were used. These last two laws especially influence jewelry, kachina dolls, pottery, weavings, and other contemporary items.

I have tried to present the laws in a simple manner, but I am not an attorney and cannot give legal advice. However, I do advise you to check your local, state, and federal agencies about laws that may apply to your collection.

There are two active trade associations to help collectors, dealers, and other groups that you may wish to join or use as an information source. Both are listed in chapter 9, General Information, of this book.

Panamint Shoshone basket

2

NATIVE AMERICAN BASKETS

HISTORY

Baskets is one of the art forms most sought after by collectors of American Indian artifacts. The charm of these irreplaceable old baskets lies in their beauty, historic importance, laborious construction, and scarcity.

Baskets are as old as the creativity of humankind. The need for containers in which to carry, store, and cook things made construction of baskets from the vegetation in their environment a necessity for early humans. Baskets were constructed by all the native peoples, as evidenced by remnants and whole baskets that have been found at sites attributed to the Mound Builders and the Southwest prehistoric peoples, as well as among the native cultures of the Northeast, Northwest, and Western United States. The prehistoric peoples of the Southwest are known as the Basket Makers, because archaeological finds at their burial sites revealed their prolific use of baskets.

Collectible Native American baskets were made by tribes from various parts of the United States and Canada. Among the Western states, California, the Southwest, and the Northwest Pacific Coast provide the greatest quality and quantity of American Indian baskets.

American Indian baskets were made by the women of the tribe. What is truly astonishing is the attractive, clean art created by these women given the bleak and often dirty conditions in which they worked. The women constructed the baskets using only natural materials from the earth around them, and using only a bone awl and flint knife as tools. (Later, in the 1800s, metal awls and knives were used, and better facilities were available.) Also remarkable is the fact that the elaborate designs found on these baskets were created in a woman's mind and executed stitch by stitch, without ever drawing up a plan. Few artists have worked under such conditions and provided us with such great art.

Baskets were made for use, for sale, and for barter among the American Indians well before the invasion of the Europeans. However, historically (1700s–1800s) baskets were traded by the American Indians with the Spanish, English, and French explorers. This led to the American Indians making baskets specifically for trade and eventually for sale. Nearly all baskets made prior to 1850, with rare exceptions, were destroyed through native use.

BASKET TYPES

American Indian women made many different sizes and shapes of baskets. However, they always made them in a traditional way. Early baskets were made for utilitarian purposes only. Examples are:

baby cradles	hats
bags	mats
burden baskets	mortar hoppers
children's toys	seed containers
clothing	sifters
cooking vessels	storage containers
gambling trays	water containers
gifts and ceremonial baskets	winnowing trays

Most of the baskets made after 1890 (except for some made for tribal ceremonial use) were made to sell to collectors and tourists. Baskets made after 1890 and up to the present provide the bulk of what is collected today.

Examples of the fine early baskets are the feathered baskets of the California Pomo tribe, the bottleneck baskets and gambling trays of the California/Tulare/Yokut tribe, the ollas of the Arizona Apache tribe, and the fine baskets of the California Panamint tribe.

The desire to produce a basket that would sell to the collectors heavily influenced the types of American Indian baskets produced. These more contemporary baskets consist of the usual types plus the following:

animal figures	purses
covered bottles	sewing kits
cups and saucers	teapots
fishing creels	vases
miniatures	wall pockets
pedestal baskets	whatnots

Some of the highest-quality collectible baskets were produced during this period. In the early 1900s magnificent California Washoe baskets were woven by such artists as Dat-So-La-Lee (Louise Keyser), Lizzie Peters, Tillie Snooks, Sarah Mayo, Maggie James, and Lena Dick. The great California Yosemite Valley baskets produced by Miwok, Paiute, and Mono tribes are typified by such artists as Tina Charli, Lucy Telles, Lena Tom, and Maggie Howard, to list a few. There are too many to mention, but a flavoring of the artists helps the collector realize that each basket had a maker of importance.

During the late 1800s and the early 1990s thousands of baskets that are considered to be prime collectible baskets were made. By the latter half of this century American Indian basket weavers stopped making baskets, and many did not pass on the knowledge to their relatives. The decline in both quality and quantity took place due to a combination of factors, including a relocation of the American Indians to areas where basket materials were not available, jobs paying more than those within the society, and encroachment by modern civilization into areas where materials for the American Indian baskets were once gathered.

CONSTRUCTION OF BASKETS

To understand American Indian baskets, one needs to know a little about the construction of the basket. By understanding the construction and materials used, the collector will be able to better identify the tribe, tell if repairs have been made, and distinguish a foreign-made piece from the authentic American Indian basket.

First, the American Indian woman and members of her family had to harvest the materials used; there was no hobby store in which to purchase the construction materials. Each tribe used the natural materials available in its area. Therefore, the materials used offer a clue as to the tribe of the weaver. Examples of a few of the many plant materials used are willow, sedge, cane, birch bark, juncas, sumac, tule, Joshua tree root, bulrush (tule), bracken fern root, grasses, devil's claw, hazelnut, redbud, rabbitbrush, wild currant, and cottonwood; a few of the nonvegetative materials incorporated into American Indian baskets are ivory, baleen (from the whale's mouth), bird feathers, quills, shells, hematite, tar, earthen paints, wool, buttons, beads, seal gut, and hide; you name it, and it was more than likely used.

After patiently collecting the material, the gatherers had to splice, shred, and sometimes pound it into the basic form needed for weaving. Sizing of the spliced pieces was necessary to make the stitching even. In the early years this was done by an American Indian woman pulling the material between her front teeth. In later years the top of a tin can was perforated, and the splice of material was pulled through the different-sized holes to create the needed size. After the material was harvested at just the right time, it had to be cured for approximately one year from harvest before a basket could be started. The curing period varied from material to material and from tribe to tribe. The tool most needed to make a basket was the awl, which is a large pointed needle used to make holes, so that the stitching could be pulled through the working area of the basket.

When studying weaving, one needs to know that a warp is the strand that runs vertically in the basket and the weft is the strand that runs horizontally.

The main methods of construction used were coiling, twining, splinting, and plaiting. Coiling consists of sewing a flexible material over a spiraling foundation. The foundation can be rods, grasses, or a combination of both. Knowing the foundation material will help you identify coiled baskets, since most are varied in terms of the foundation as well as the types of stitching that were used. The sewing strands are produced from splitting and sizing the flexible materials collected for this purpose, such as willow, juncas, and so on. Stitches are the individually whipped or sewn fibers that join the coils together. The fag end (the untwisted end of the coiling material) is inserted into a hole made by the awl. The hole can be made so that the stitching material goes through or around and underneath the coil in a variety of ways. Coils consist of bundles of grass or small sticks, single rods, rods combined with grass or two or three rods stacked together horizontally, vertically, or in a triangular pile. The coils can be held together by:

1. encircling both the new coil and the previous coil.
2. encircling the new coil and just piercing the previous coil.
3. encircling the new and previous coil but interlocking with the stitch on the previous coil.
4. encircling the new coil and interlocking with the stitch on the previous coil while only piercing the old coil.
5. encircling the new coil, interlocking, splitting, and encircling the previous coil.
6. encircling the new coil, interlocking, splitting, and piercing the previous coil (diagram 1).

One of the diagnostic tools for identifying a coiled basket is to determine the direction of the stitching. The stitching order can be either to the weaver's left or right. The direction of construction is found by first determining the working face of the basket (the side most finished) and then by examining the face to determine the stitching direction. How can direction play a role in determining the tribe that made the basket? For example, in California baskets those stitched to the right (clockwise) were

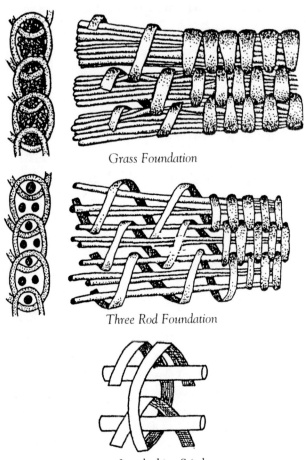

Grass Foundation

Three Rod Foundation

Interlocking Stitch

End Stitch   Beginning Stitch

Non-Interlocking Stitch

Diagram 1. Basket coiling techniques

made by Southern California tribes, and all that go to the left (counter-clockwise) are from Northern California (with a few exceptions). So, for identification purposes, if a basket is stitched to the right, you can eliminate many Northern California tribes.

It is sometimes hard to see the foundation material on a finished coiled basket due to the tight stitching. The best method for viewing the foundation is to use a magnifying glass to peek in at the material. A grass foundation creates a wide and flexible coil. Single-rod coiled baskets will feel and look flat, while three-rod baskets have a small, fine, wavy texture going around the basket. The finishing on the rim of a basket can also be used to help identify baskets.

While the weaver worked on the foundation construction and stitching, she mentally figured out the design. Some designs are known to have been passed down from mother to daughter, showing that not all designs were created on the spot. This was the hard part of making the basket, as she had to fit the design to the size and shape of the basket while working on it.

Twining is another method used in the construction of baskets. In twining, two or more flexible weft strands are worked between vertical warps. Numerous combinations of warp and weft weaving can be achieved. Types of twining include plain, wrap, lattice, and three-strand. The twining technique produces a soft, flexible type of basket (diagram 2).

As with coiled baskets, the construction methods and materials used in twined baskets will give you clues as to which American Indian tribe made the basket. Northern California tribes were prolific weavers of twined baskets. The Attu baskets of Alaska are also fine examples of grass-twined baskets.

In plaiting, the warp and weft are interwoven at right angles to one another. Usually the warp and weft are similar in size, flexibility, and appearance. An exception is wicker plaiting in which the warps are usually different from the weft strands. Examples of plaiting are plain (checkerboard-appearing), twill, double twill, curlicue, and lattice. The weaving in plaiting can be closed tightly or open (where you can see between the warps and weft) (diagram 3).

Diagonal Twining

Three Strand Twining

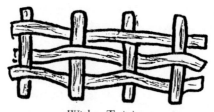

Wicker Twining

Simple Twining

Diagram 2. Basket twining techniques

Studying the weave, materials used, finish, and design of the basket will help in identifying it. However, coiled and plaited baskets of the Pennsylvania Germans are similar to the large Papago coiled containers and plaited Eastern Algonquian baskets. The Ozark, Shaker, and Appalachian baskets also resemble American Indian plaited baskets.

Plaited wood-splint baskets appear to have originated among the early Europeans. Prehistoric evidence of this distinct method of construction is absent from the continent, although fragments of baskets displaying other European techniques are evident, showing that the American Indians borrowed from the Europeans to produce baskets with materials and designs that were familiar to them.

Before the arrival of the Europeans, most American Indian baskets had little or no design because they were made strictly for use. The designs used by the American Indian weavers were always traditional; therefore, knowledge about design is another tool that can be used to identify a basket's tribe. Designs were predominately geometrical.

IDENTIFYING YOUR BASKETS

It is vitally important to be able to identify baskets if you want to evaluate their value properly, though it is not really difficult to get a general handle on identifying most American Indian baskets. I have already alluded to most of the methods used to identify the source of a given basket, including looking at the construction, material, and design of the basket. By following these few steps, identification is made easier:

1. Give the basket a general visual once-over to determine that it is American Indian. To do so, check that the:
    a. materials are of North American origin.
    b. general size and shape of the baskets are typical for those woven by tribes of North America.
    c. construction is American Indian.

Diagram 3. Basket plaiting techniques

2. Determine the type of construction. To do so, consider:
    a. whether the basket is coiled, twined, or plaited.
    b. what material is used for stitching, bundles, and plaiting.
    c. what direction the stitching takes (on coiled baskets only).

3. Make sure the design is traditional.

4. Examine the fineness of the work; this will direct you to characteristics of American Indian tribes that did extra fine weaving.

5. Refer to the tribes given in the basket guide. For each tribe listed, the guide provides information on the type of construction, materials, and workmanship.

To learn the materials, however, one must spend time with collectors, dealers, and in museums examining as many baskets as possible. After awhile, many baskets become easily identified by casual examination, though some are difficult even for the advanced collector or curator.

COLLECTING AMERICAN INDIAN BASKETS

The true collector of American Indian baskets collects for the enjoyment of the hobby rather than for investment in the market. However, the market on American Indian baskets has been on a steady increase.

There are more and more American Indian basket collectors coming into the hobby each year, and there are fewer old baskets available than ever before.

Antique American Indian baskets can be found for sale at the following places:

American Indian dealers	estate sales
American Indian shows	flea markets
antique shows	other collectors' homes
antique stores	yard sales

To expand your opportunities to find a good basket, tell your friends, local merchants, and neighbors that you are a collector of American Indian baskets. You will be surprised at where the baskets show up. Remember,

An example of grading baskets on a scale of 1 to 5, one being best.

	1	2	3	4	5
Fineness of work Stitching Form Craftmanship	Very fine (Examples: Pomo & Panamint, should be 35-45 stitches per inch)	Good	Average	Poor	Wide and irregular spacing, bad form, bad work
Design Balance of figures Quality of artwork	Excellent	Good	Average	Poor	Poor
Tribal tradition Design Construction Materials Form	True in all aspects	True	True	Meets most criteria	Design, material or construction is wrong
Condition Stitches Rim Body Color & Brightness	Excellent	Good Minor breakage, 1-2 missing stitches in rim or body	Average rim and/or body, some damage	Rim stitches missing or broken, light damage or stains to body	Rim breakage, serious damage or stains to body

Diagram 4. Grading system for baskets

American Indian women were very prolific weavers and there are still thousands of old baskets waiting to be found. Some serious collectors even run want ads in periodicals. The adventure of seeking out baskets is very rewarding.

BUYING AMERICAN INDIAN BASKETS

The first rule is to purchase the best quality basket that you can afford. Quality is determined by the following:

1. Fineness of workmanship (35–50 stitches per inch is very good)
2. Good balance in the design
3. Pleasing shape and size
4. Excellent condition

The price to pay for the basket should be on or very near the market value. The market value is determined by what is being paid for comparable baskets. Using this as a guide as well as auction prices, dealer prices, and other trade sources will aid you in paying an appropriate price.

When buying, select the type of American Indian basket that satisfies you. Your particular desires and your display space limitations may determine size, shape, and designs you collect. Always be sure that the basket is an American Indian basket and is true to the tribe to which it is attributed, then proceed with checking the quality and condition. A basket in good condition will have few or no stitches missing, no rim breaks, a clean surface with no stains, a bright design, and a good shape.

Diagram 4 provides a simple grading standard to assist you in determining the quality of the basket. It uses numbers from one (best) to five (worst) to give the collector a quick reference to quality.

Intermediate and advanced collectors avoid certain types of baskets, causing them to be harder to sell and less desirable to collect. For example, baskets with pedestal bases, wall pockets, and mats are not very collectible because they are considered too Victorian. On the other hand, a combination of tight weave (35-50 stitches per inch), great design (geometrical or zoomorphic), traditional shapes, and good condition is what makes for what is known in the trade as a great basket. The following tribes are known for their great baskets: Pomo, Chemehuevi, Panamint, Kawaiisu, Tulare/Yokuts, Miwok, Apache, Tubatulabal, Pima, Washoe, and Paiute.

Basket sales were covered in the opening chapter of this book; however, when purchasing your basket, try to keep in mind that someday you, or someone for you, will have to sell the basket you are buying. Therefore, it is best to purchase and collect good, marketable baskets, meaning baskets that other collectors will want to purchase.

Trading is a good way to acquire baskets. Many collectors will not sell you one of their baskets. However, if you can bring them one they want badly enough, they may trade for it. Most dealers take trade-ins if you wish to upgrade your collection.

TAKING CARE OF YOUR BASKETS

Displaying your collection of baskets where you and others can enjoy their beauty is important. Glass cases are the best type of display, as they keep the baskets out of reach of dust, insects, pests, and small children, while still allowing the baskets to be viewed. In some homes, shelving will suffice to display your baskets.

Never glue or nail baskets to the walls or shelves. Some collectors place a nail through the center of a basket to fasten it to a wall, but this produces a small hole that damages the basket. To display large tray-shaped baskets, use plastic or wire display stands available through your local antique dealer.

The most commonly asked question about the storage of baskets is whether humidity or temperature has any effect on the baskets. Unless the humidity is very high which allows mold to develop on the basket, there is no concern. Cold weather has no effect, but very hot climates will dry out the fibers. Usually, if the basket is not left in direct sunlight, moderately high temperature has no effect. If your baskets are drying out, periodic misting of water in the air around the basket will help.

If your baskets must be stored, carefully pack them in strong containers.

Wrap and separate each basket with clean white tissue, and do not use newspaper as the ink can adhere to baskets if moisture is present. Also, do not use sealed plastic bags to store your baskets in, as moisture can build up inside them and mold will result.

Insects that like to chew on wood will damage baskets. Be sure to keep your baskets free from any type of insect. Mothballs placed in cabinets or storage areas help, as does the careful use of insect spray. You can also use a more natural way of defeating these pesky insects by placing bay leaf, allspice, and/or cinnamon sticks in the baskets. At any sign of termites, silverfish, or other pests, remove the baskets and relocate to a safe area.

Rodents and pets have been known to damage baskets. A very fine Apache basket was partly eaten by a collector's pet parrot, and the rim of a fine Chumash basket was greatly enjoyed by another's dog.

People cause most of the damage done to baskets by improper handling and use. Storing baskets too close to a fireplace or heater can darken or burn a basket. I have seen a $10,000 Apache olla auctioned for $300 because it had been used for storing firewood next to a fireplace so that one entire side of the large basket was charred black. Most damage is caused by improper lifting. Grabbing the rim with one hand can often break or weaken the rim. The proper way to pick up a basket is with both hands at the same time— one hand under the basket and one hand near the edge to balance it. Never set baskets where large objects can push against them or drop onto them.

Baskets often appear on the market with ink stains, cigarette burns, and other marks caused by careless usage. There is usually no way to remove stains.

Cleaning of baskets can be done by the collector. Dust can be removed with a soft brush. Dirt or film can be removed by careful use of water and a mild liquid soap applied with a toothbrush. Use a dry towel to blot out any excess moisture and let the basket dry naturally out of direct sunlight. Sometimes stitches will burst when a basket is cleaned with water. If you are concerned about cleaning your baskets, there are experts who can clean as well as repair them.

Are American Indian baskets commonly repaired? The answer is no, as it is expensive to have the work done. The owner of a damaged basket must weigh the costs of repair against the total value of the basket after it is repaired. A very valuable basket may well be worth hundreds of dollars of repair work to bring it back to its full value.

Caring for your baskets includes keeping records of them. Data about the history, costs, and tribe are often neglected. The following should be recorded:

date of construction	name of weaver
description	price paid
name of previous owner	tribe

With the handiness of video photography, I also recommend that you make a videotape of your collection. In the case of loss, there is no better way to describe your baskets to the insurance adjuster and authorities; plus it is fun to sit back and view your collection via video with others.

THE AMERICAN INDIAN BASKET MARKET

The price of collectible American Indian baskets has been increasing from the first day they were made to sell to the tourist and collector. The large increase in values for antique baskets has occurred during the past 20–30 years. You will hear of some great baskets doubling in price in 12 months or less, but these baskets are few and hard to find. True, there are investors in the market, because the good return on investment has attracted a few people who are in it only for the money, but most baskets are bought and sold by the "true collectors." Fortunately, large investors have not taken the basket market to the levels seen in paintings, sculptures, and other art forms. Would not that take all the fun out of collecting? Good basket buys are still out there: every year collectors find exceptional pieces from old estates, collections, American Indian shows, dealers, auctions, flea markets, neighbors, and other places. The hunt for good collectibles is half the fun.

The market increases are smaller in the lesser-quality baskets. Most beginner collectors find that baskets with lower cost and of lesser quality have good availability and so start by collecting these.

How valuable are American Indian baskets? A good Washoe basket made by the famous weaver Dat-So-La-Lee has brought in six figures. A Hupa-type basket by Elizabeth Hitchcock can bring $35,000 or more. A fine Apache olla with animal figures brought $45,000 in the early 1990s. Most baskets sell in a much lower price range as the average quality is lower. Great baskets usually bring $3,000 to $20,000, while beginner-collector baskets are valued in the hundreds of dollars.

REPRODUCTIONS

Of all the types of American Indian artifacts, basket collectors have the least chance of purchasing reproductions. Except for the attempts by the African and Pakistani weavers to produce a basket similar to the American Indian ones, there is little risk of acquiring a reproduction. Novice collectors may get into trouble where foreign-made baskets are similar to American Indian ones; these must be closely examined in order to distinguish them from American Indian baskets. African baskets look a little like the California Mission basket but are made of the wrong materials. The construction is also different.

Pakistani baskets are similar to Navajo wedding baskets, but again the wrong materials and dyes are used. The Brazilians make a basket that looks like a large gathering basket of a Northern California tribe, but here again the materials and workmanship are different. The Filipinos have a tightly woven basket that can be confused for an Aleut basket, but a closer look will verify the difference between the grasses: the Philippine materials have a more plastic look. As earlier mentioned, Ozark, Shaker, and Appalachian baskets can be confused for North American Indian plaited baskets quite easily.

OTHER BASKET FORMS

Other forms of baskets include corn husk items, soft twined bags, schoolhouse baskets, mats, and Great Lakes twined bags. Corn husk bags of the Northwest were made by the tribes east of the Cascades because they wanted a carrying bag flexible enough to use on their horses. The bags are flat, rectangular-shaped, and open at the top.

The earlier made bags (1800s) are of twisted hemp or willow bark materials with bear grass in its natural colors of white, yellow, and green used to decorate. After the influence of white settlers, corn husk and cotton twine were incorporated into the weaving, thus the name *corn husk bags*. The construction is simple twining and the details are false embroidery. The Nez Perce and Yakima are known for the corn husk hat that looks like a fez. Round, soft twined bags were also made as carrying containers.

The Iroquois Indians are the makers of corn husk masks. The methods of construction are twined and coiled braids, but less than 5 percent are made by the twining method.

Schoolhouse baskets are a name for the hundreds of raffia-made baskets produced by white women under the tutorage of George Wharton James. James is the author of *Indian Basketry and How to Make Indian and Other Baskets* (1903). In collecting, you will often run into these baskets. They are interesting to study but have not yet been collected very seriously.

Mats were common in the Northwest and Great Lakes areas. Today, there are few mats available to collect due to their deterioration from usage.

IDENTIFICATION GUIDE TO AMERICAN INDIAN BASKETS

The identification guide which follows lists baskets first by geographical region, then alphabetically by the tribes within each region. I have tried to include the most collectible cultures. A description of each basket is given followed by clues to its identification and a detailed discussion of its construction including the materials used. All baskets are considered to be in good condition and dated from the late 1890s to the early 1940s.

SOUTHWEST BASKETS

Hualapais

Between 1900 and 1940 the Hualapais made very utilitarian types of traditional baskets as well as finely coiled ones. Clues: Look for twined, coarse, bowl-shaped baskets with rims that are distinctly thick and flat on the upper surface.

Construction and Materials
Coiling method: Foundation materials include three-rod coils of sumac or willow. Stitching materials include splints of sumac or willow, with martynia (black devil's claw) used for designs. Later, some commercially dyed splints and raffia were also used for the designs.
Twining method: Diagonal or twill of split sumac decorated with aniline dye.

Havasupai

Havasupai coiled baskets resemble those of the Western Apache and Yavapai. The main difference is that the designs of the Havasupai are massive, and there are fewer design elements. Also, the rims were often done in tan willow splints instead of martynia. Clues: The twined baskets, like the Hualapais, are easily recognized once you have seen one. They are plain-looking with banded design, whereas the coiled baskets are usually fine and Apache-like.

Construction and Materials
Coiling method: Foundation material used is three-rod coils of willow. The stitching material is spliced willow.
Twining method: Closed, plain, and diagonal using acacia, willow, or cottonwood.

Hopi

Hopi baskets are easily recognized. They are large bundled coil baskets and fine wirelike wicker baskets that have brightly dyed designs of geometric, animal, and ceremonial objects. Clues: Look for the large bundled coil baskets of the Second Mesa and the fine wicker baskets of the First Mesa; both are usually very bright in color when newer but tend to fade as they age.

Construction and Materials
Coiling method: Foundation materials include large bundles of galleta grass or yucca. Stitching materials include yucca strands.

Wicker-plaited: Rabbitbrush is used for the weft with sumac, willow, or wild currant used for the warp. The rim is wrapped with yucca.

Twilled-plaited: Yucca with sumac or willow is used to strengthen the basket.

Jicarilla Apache

The Apache basket collector will see large, heavily coiled baskets where the originally dyed bright colors have faded. The pitched water jugs will be pitched only on the inside, with white clay on the outside.

Construction and Materials

Coiling method: Foundation materials include predominately five rods with some three rods of willow or sumac. Stitching materials include sumac or willow.

Twining method: These baskets are plain with some yucca used.

Mescolero Apache

The Mescolero made a coarse basket with large flat coils due to stacking three rods on top of each other. Clues: Look for star or flower designs as these were the most commonly used.

Construction and Materials

Coiling method: Foundation materials include three rods of flat coils of willow. There are also two rods with bundles. Stitches are interlocked of split yucca.

Twining method: Closed, plain, using cottonwood.

Navajo

The Navajo mainly make one type of basket, which is a tray. Clues: Look for rims with a herringbone finish on coiled baskets. Circular designs will have gaps in them to let out the spirit (*shipapu*). After 1900 most of the sacred meal baskets were made for the Navajos by the Paiutes or Utes.

Construction and Materials

Coiling method: Foundations include two rods of aromatic sumac with bundles. Materials used for coiling is yucca. Stitching is a noninterlocked split on a nonworking surface. Twining method: 2 by 2 interval twill of sumac or willow.

Papago

The Papago tribe is located in South Central Arizona. Clues: Look for big coils stitched with spliced yucca.

Construction and Materials

Coiling method: Foundation materials include bundles of yucca, cattail, or grass. Stitching is of split yucca with black devil's claw used for design.

Plaiting methods: Twill plaiting using split leaves of sotol.

Pima

The Pimas made fine baskets. Clues: You can tell a Pima from a similar-looking Papago basket by the willow stitches of the Pima vs. the yucca stitches of the Papago basket. Pima baskets, like some Apache baskets, have a black start and rim. However, Apache baskets differ from the Pima's inasmuch as willow rod bundles were used for coils.

Construction and Materials

Coiling method: Foundation materials include bundles of grass stems. Stitching material is willow.

Pueblo baskets

A number of the Arizona and New Mexico Pueblos made baskets, but they are not baskets considered to be the better of the collectible pieces. They are usually utilitarian with open weaves of wicker construction and are plaited.

San Juan: open weave wicker
San Ildefonso: twill-plaited
Jemez: twill-plaited
Zuni: wicker

San Carlos Apache

Baskets shaped as ollas and dishes with dog, horse, and human designs were beautifully made by the San Carlos Apache. Clues: You can tell a similar-looking Pima basket from an Apache basket—even though they both have the same stitching—by examining the difference in the coiling material: Apache baskets have willow rods, and Pima baskets have bundles of grass.

Construction and Materials
Coiling method: Foundation materials include three rods of willow and occasionally mulberry. Stitching materials include willow with devil's claw for design.
Twining method: Plain and diagonal use of three strands of twining with the use of squawberry. Occasionally sumac was used.
Wicker plaiting: Willow was used.

White Mountain Apache

The White Mountain Apache made exceptional ollas and bowls. Some pieces can be worth twice what the average pieces bring. Clues: These baskets have a black center start and a black rim, as do the San Carlos baskets.

Construction and Materials
Coiling method: Foundation materials include three rods of willow. Stitching materials include willow with devil's claw for the black design.
Twining method: Closed plain and diagonal use of mulberry.

Yavapai

Yavapai baskets are high-quality Apache baskets and are similar to the San Carlos and White Mountain Apache. Clues: The Yavapai emphasize large black negative areas of martynia and smaller geometric elements than the San Carlos or White Mountain Apache.

Construction and Materials
Coiling method: Foundation materials include three rods of willow or cottonwood. Stitching materials include willow, devil's claw, and red yucca or Joshua tree root.

Northwest, Canada, and Alaska baskets

Athabascan
These baskets are often unidentified and left behind by the collector. Clues: They look like single-rod baskets and usually have a dark patination and no decoration.

Construction and Materials
Coiling method: The foundation material used is a single rod of willow. Stitching is spaced and includes conifer root. It may be decorated but is usually left plain. There is some use of colored bark or quill.

Chilcotin
This very unique Northwest basket features a rod running below its rim on its burden baskets. Clues: Look for four zones of design, with three equal in width below the carrying rod.

Construction and Materials
Coiling method: Foundation materials include rounded coils of peeled cedar root. Decoration is imbrication with white and red cherry designs.

Nez Perce
The Nez Perce made mainly corn husk bags. Clue: The designs on the front and back differ from one another.

Construction and Materials
Twining Method: Closed, plain, and wrapped warp of hemp and grass stem. Weft of corn husk, hemp, willow, cherry, cotton twine, or rush. Decoration materials include corn husk and grass-dyed overlays, with colored wool and false embroidery.

Nootka

The many small round- and oval-lidded tourist baskets are very economical and collectible. Clues: The bottom of the basket has a start that is a square of checker-woven cedar bark, and the wrapped twining always inclines to the right.

Construction and Materials
Twining method: Three strands of open, plain, and closed wrap. Twining materials include cedar bark, bear grass, and root of spruce.
Plaiting method: Open, cross-warped of cedar bark or cattail. Decoration is made of aniline-dyed grasses and the occasional use of whale skin.

Makah

The Makah tribe is found around Cape Flattery located in Northern Washington. They made very fine baskets, which are sought after by collectors in the Northwestern United States. Clues: Makah and Nootka baskets have as a start a square of checker that is of woven cedar bark, and the wrapped twining always inclines to the right.

Construction and Materials
Twining method: Open and closed wrap of cedar bark and bear grass with a wrapped weft.
Plaiting method: 2 by 2 twill. Decoration includes designs done with wrapped twining and dyed grasses.

Tlingit

This tribe is from the upper Northwest Coast. They made very fine colorful baskets. Clues: These baskets are thin-walled and finely woven, usually in bright red, orange, brown, and yellow colors.

Construction and Materials
Twining method: Open and closed, using various types of twining even in the same basket. Materials include spruce root, maidenhair fern, and bear grass.
Plain plaiting method: Material used is cedar bark.

Thompson River (Salish)

The Thompson River Indians made a strong, beautiful basket. Clue: Look for much imbrication using the entire wall in the design.

Construction and Materials
Coiling method: Foundation materials include bundles and splint coils of roots from cedar, spruce, or juniper.
Coiling is to the left. The base slats of the basket are of cedar.
Twining method: Open plain and closed plain with the spruce root or cedar stick diagonal.
Plaiting method: Materials include grasses, bulrush, or tule. Decorations were made by imbrication of cherry bark and sometimes black and red beading overlay. Purple grass was used in the Upper Thompson River area.

Wasco

The Wasco Indians are known as the makers of the famous *Sally Bags*. Clues: Look for flexible bags with designs of animals and skeletal motifs as well as geometric designs in their baskets.

Construction and Materials
Twining method: Closed wrap of wild Indian hemp with corn husk, hemp, or grasses as weft. Decorations are made with the colors from the above materials with some trade beads woven in; sometimes the edges are lined with cloth and leather.

Aleut

There are two very fine woven types to consider collecting here: the beautiful Attu and the Atka from the Aleutian Islands. Clues: Look for very fine silky grass baskets. There are some with lids and some with open rim work.

Construction and Materials
Twining method: Closed and open plain on those of the Attu. They only make use of three strand twining with rye grass as the material.

Eskimo

These baskets are beautiful. Clues: Look for large coils covered with grass stitching. They are often beehive in shape and may be lidded.

Construction and Materials
Coiling method: Foundation materials include bundles of grass, with coiling to the left and single rod with coils of willow or spruce root.
Twining method: Closed or open with parallel warp elements; the rim is braided. Decoration materials include dyed seal gut and dyed grasses.

SOUTHEAST BASKETS

Cherokee

The Cherokee made a nice plaited basket in various forms which are different in both North Carolina and Oklahoma. Clue: Hickory bark is almost always wrapped on the rims.

Construction and Materials
Plaiting, plain: Material used is oak splints in North Carolina.
Twill plaiting: In North Carolina the material used is river cane.
Wicker: In Oklahoma river cane is used.

Choctaw

The Mississippi and Oklahoma Choctaw made a nice plaited basket. Clue: The oak splint tells you the basket is from Mississippi.

Construction and Materials
Twill plaiting: Materials include cane stem splints with some white oak used. Decoration was made by dying cane red or black.

Coushatta (Koasati)

The Coushatta made a nice coiled pine needle basket. Clue: Look for the raffia stitching.

Construction and Materials

Coiling method: Foundation material used is bundles of pine needles. The simple stitching is of raffia.

Plaiting method: Twill, using split swamp cane or white oak splints.

Houma

This is a Louisiana-made basket which is very unique today. Clues: Look for the stitching that produces a very different basket with large slanted bundled-up stitching with no color decoration.

Construction and Materials

Coiling method: Foundation materials used are bundles of split palmetto leaves. The Houma used a unique spacing called a loop stitch.

Plaiting method: The material used is cane.

Seminole

The Seminole made pine needle and sweet grass baskets. Clue: Look for colored thread on both the pine needle and sweet grass baskets.

Construction and Materials

Coiling method: Foundation materials include bundles of pine needles or sweet grass. Stitching materials include twine or colored cotton thread.

Plaiting method: Twill is open and closed cane with palmetto fan.

NORTHEAST BASKETS

Chippewa

The Chippewa made many fine baskets. Clue: Look for a fine birch bark basket.

Construction and Materials

Coiling method: Foundation materials include bundles of sweet grass or single rod.

Plaiting method: Plain, made of black oak.
Wicker method: Willow is the material used. Decorations
were made using dyed splints, curl twists, and by the etching
of birch bark and by quill.

Nipmuc

This tribe is from Massachusetts and Connecticut and made beautiful
baskets with side handles. Clue: Look for use of dots as outlines.

Construction and Materials
Plaiting, plain: The material used is oak splints. Any
decoration is done with paints.

WESTERN BASKETS: CALIFORNIA AND NEVADA

Northern California

Hupa, Karok, and Yurok

I have grouped these three tribes together due to the similarity in basket
making and tribal location. Clues: Although all three tribes are very similar,
Karok baskets use willow for the warp and have more red in the decoration.

Construction and Materials
Twining method: Open and closed plain twining with a half
twist overlay of decoration. The Hupa and Yurok used hazel
for the warp. The Hupa used willow, alder, cottonwood,
pine, redwood, and grape for the weft. The Yurok used pine,
redwood, and spruce in weft construction. The Karok used
pine, willow, alder, and cottonwood in the weft. Decoration
was accomplished by using a colored half-twist overlay with
bear grass, maidenhair fern, and elder.

Maidu

Maidu have a very distinct look of their own. Clues: Look for elaborate use
of redbud in their designs, and sometimes the rim is of alternating red and tan.

Construction and Materials
Coiling method: Foundation materials include three rods of
willow or peeled redbud. Occasionally baskets were made

with only one rod. Stitching was done with a split stitch on the inside and interlocking coils to the left made of spliced willow, redbud, and bracken fern root.

Twining method: Open and closed plain and diagonal with materials of maple or willow; the weft is of redbud, willow, or fir.

Miwok

Some of the great Yosemite Valley baskets of the 1920s were made by this tribe. Clue: Note the interlocking stitch on the outside of the working surface.

Construction and Materials

Coiling method: Foundation materials include three bunched rods, some single-rod baskets of willow with the foundation being of sumac or deer grass in the Southern Miwok area. Stitching is interlocking to the left. Materials include redbud, bracken fern, split willow, and sedge root.

Twining method: Plain warp and weft of willow or hazel.

Modoc

This tribe made its home in North Central California. Clue: Look for soft-walled, floppy, dark brown baskets with very little decoration.

Construction and Materials

Twining method: Plain of brown tule rush (both the warp and the weft). When decoration is done it is accomplished by the use of grass overlay and bird quill dyed yellow.

Mono

This tribe lives in both California and Nevada. Clue: To tell a Mono basket from a Tulare/Yokut, note that the Mono is stitched to the left, while the Tulare/Yokut is stitched to the right.

Construction and Materials

Coiling method: Foundation materials include grass bundles with some single- and some three-rod baskets being made. The coiling of willow and sumac is to the left with noninterlocking materials of sedge, willow, and bracken fern root.

Twining method: Open twining and closed diagonal.

Pitt River

This tribe was located in northeastern California. Clues: Look for a full-twist overlay and more elaborate designs, with the designs showing both on the inside and outside of the basket.

Construction and Materials
Twining method: Plain warp of willow splints and a weft of pine root and rush. Decoration is done with a full-twist overlay of bear grass, redbud, and black fern.

Pomo

This is a very finely woven basket with many distinct qualities that help to identify it. Clues: In addition to being finely woven, Pomo baskets are quite often elaborately decorated with shell beads, glass beads, and feathers.

Construction and Materials
Coiling method: Foundation materials include three rods that are piled in a triangular way and a single rod of willow or hazel. Stitching materials include an interlocking stitch of sedge root, bulrush, and bracken fern, with stitching to the left.

Twining method: Open and closed plain, twill, lattice, and three-strand braiding or plaiting techniques are employed. Materials include willow for the warp, sedge root for the weft, with bracken fern and redbud for the color design.

Shasta

This is a finely designed twined basket. Clues: The full-twist overlay decoration will show on the inside and outside of the basket; the half twist will only show on the working surface of the basket.

Construction and Materials
Twining method: Closed and open plain twining of willow or hazel for the warp, with the weft of yellow pine or tule

root. Decoration is accomplished through a full-twist overlay of bear grass, maidenhair fern, and some quill. Beads, paint, and feathers are also used. The design is usually of geometric patterns in bands and simple motifs.

Central and Southern California baskets

Chumash

Chumash baskets are one of the oldest and rarest of the North American Indian baskets. Clues: Look for the two types of coils to be sure it is Chumash. These baskets look similar to the Mission baskets except for the information on the coils. The Chumash have a jump stitch on the non-working surface of the basket. The jump stitch is the fag (slanting end) of the previous stitch tucked into the next stitch.

Construction and Materials
Coiling method: Foundation materials include both grass and rods in the same basket which is unique to the Chumash. The start of the basket will be done in coils of rods, the finish in bundles of juncas. The coils go to the right. Stitching material includes interlocking stitches of split juncas or sumac.
Twining method: Closed plain, with the warps of juncas or willow and the weft of juncas, tule rush, or sumac. Decoration is sometimes accomplished with dyed split sumac.

Kawaiisu

This is a small tribe located near the Tehachapi Pass who made very fine baskets. Clue: The Kawaiisu did not use redbud, sedge, or juncas in their baskets.

Construction and Materials
Coiling method: Foundation material includes grass bundles, with coiling to the right. Stitching materials include split willow, Joshua tree root, bracken fern root, and devil's claw.

Mission

There are many subcultures of the Mission Indians, but all their baskets are similar in construction. Clues: Look for the jump stitch on the nonworking side of the basket. Juncas is the main material used.

Construction and Materials

Coiling method: Foundation material includes grass bundles with coiling to the right. Stitching material includes interlocking stitches of juncas or sumac with some desert palm and tule rush.

Twining method: Plain with warp materials of sumac, juncas, or willow and the weft of sumac and juncas.

Tubatulabal

This is a tribe located in the mountains that drain the Kern River in San Bernardino County. Clues: At first this basket looks like the Tulare/Yokut, but at closer examination you will see red yucca root and devil's claw; neither is used in the construction of the Tulare/Yokut basket.

Construction and Materials

Coiling method: Foundation material is bundles of grass with coiling to the right. Stitching material includes noninterlocking stitches of willow or sedge, with yucca root and devil's claw.

Twining method: Plain; the warp and weft are of willow with open and closed weave.

Tulare/Yokut

This tribe made great baskets. Clues: Look for tight weave, rattlesnake designs, and great forms which include the bottleneck and large flaring bowls.

Construction and Materials

Coiling method: Foundation material includes grass coils, with redbud and willow. Stitching material includes noninterlocking stitches of split sedge, redbud, and bracken fern with coiling to the right.

Twining method: The warp is of willow or tule, while the

weft is of willow, conifer, redbud, or grape. Decoration is accomplished by using woodpecker and quail feathers and sometimes red wool as a fringe on the bottleneck baskets.

Washoe

This tribe is known for making some of the greatest baskets including those of Dat-So-La-Lee. Clues: Washoe coiled baskets have a fine, even-stitched look with elaborate designs.

Construction and Materials

Coiling method: Foundation materials include three rods that are stacked in a pyramidal shape or a single rod of willow. Coiling is to the left. Stitching material includes interlocking stitches of willow, bracken fern, and redbud. Single rod stitching covers two rods at a time.

Twining method: Plain and diagonal, open and closed, the warp is of willow while the weft is of bracken fern and redbud.

Nevada and Great Basin baskets

Chemehuevi

This basket is very clean-looking and is finely woven and can be easily distinguished once seen. Clues: The coiled rim has black and white alternating stitches (ticking). The design is black and simple and usually in horizontal bands.

Construction and Materials

Coiling method: Foundation material includes three rods of willow. Stitching material includes willow and devil's claw.

Twining method: Open, plain, and diagonal.

Panamint

The Panamint tribe is listed among the makers of the finest stitched baskets. Clues: Look for rims having ticking of black and white stitching. Another distinguishing characteristic is a single band of color at the bottom and again near the top of the design.

Construction and Materials

Coiling method: Foundation material includes grass bundles, three rods, and a single rod. The coiling is to the right. The rod foundation is made from willow or sumac, with bunch grass used for the grass foundation. Stitching materials include split willow, bulrush root, devil's claw, and Joshua tree root.

Paiute

The Paiute made very nice twined water jugs as well as fine coiled baskets. Clues: The Paiute always used three-rod coils, stitches are interlocking, and coiling is to the left.

Construction and Materials

Coiling method: Foundation material includes three rods of willow. Stitching materials are interlocking. Willow, bracken fern, redbud, sedge, and red yucca roots were used. Twining method: The diagonal is of willow; the weft and warp are made of sumac.

3

AMERICAN INDIAN POTTERY

HISTORY

American Indian pottery affords its collectors the opportunity to enjoy ceramics produced from primitive times until now. Pottery is one of man's earliest forms of recorded art. The Egyptians and Chinese date some of their earliest pieces back to 4000 BCE and 7000 BCE respectfully. Some of the world's most magnificent pottery pieces were made in South and Central America, and many have survived for us to enjoy. It is believed that much of the influence of pottery in the Southwestern United States came from these two regions of the world.

Fired pottery and its designs have a remarkable resistance to deterioration. As a result, archaeologists have available to them an open book of prehistoric information. Collectors also have a fresh view of American Indian designs that is uninfluenced by outsiders.

American Indians have made pottery since their arrival via the Bering Strait. Prehistoric potters created the tradition that historic and contemporary potters—coupled with their own creativity—have borrowed for many years. For prehistoric and historic pieces, the main areas of collection are the Central and Southwestern states. Contemporary production areas have been the East Coast, Midwest, and Southwestern United States.

Cochiti vase, New Mexico

Pottery is a unique collectible and charms many people into owning it because:

1. It connotates the creative work of the indigenous people that were not influenced by outsiders.
2. It has beauty of size, shape, design, and workmanship.
3. Most pieces are available and affordable.
4. One can collect a piece of the American Indian tradition.
5. Pottery gives the collector a direct feeling for the potter.
6. There is a wide variety of types of pottery from which to choose.
7. The designs are intriguing, as no one is sure of the meaning of many of the old ones.
8. Rarity plays a role for the better prehistoric and historic pieces.
9. Famous named potters in the 20th century inspire many collectors.
10. It is fun.

FAMOUS AMERICAN INDIAN POTTERS

Many American Indian potters of the 20th century will be recorded as America's great artists. The Rembrandt of American Indian potters will no doubt be Maria Martinez from the New Mexico Pueblo of San Ildefonso. This woman and her husband, Julian Martinez, originated a polished blackware pottery called black matte. This beautiful gun metal, gray-black pottery with its designs graces the homes and collections of thousands worldwide.

Maria was a prolific potter and her pieces are often found in the least expected places. Although the market values on her pieces are high, many reasonable finds have been made by collectors.

Margaret Tafoya from the Santa Clara Pueblo in New Mexico is also one of the top Southwestern Indian potters. Her work consists of black matte pottery that is beautifully carved and incised. Most of her pottery is fairly large in size.

Nampeyo of Hano and the Nampeyo family are Hopi and world famous for Nampeyo's special design style. Using the prehistoric Sikyatki pottery pieces as a model, she fashioned a beautiful squat bowl of black and red on tan. Her daughters and other members of the family have continued this distinguished style for years, and it is still very collectible today.

Lucy Lewis was an Acoma Pueblo potter known for her fine line, black-on-white and polychrome floral pieces. Her pottery is highly collectible, available, and moving upward in price.

There are hundreds of other fine pottery artists, but it would take a separate book to list them all.

AREAS OF POTTERY PRODUCTION

The Eastern United States produced prehistoric pottery as did Canada and Alaska. Eastern pottery is beautiful in its own way: tannish gray with inscribed decorations in the later stages. There were four styles from 300 BCE to 1600 BCE. Differentiations in time periods can be made by degree of art work produced, bottom shape (pointed to round), coiling, temper material used, and shape of the pot's neck.

Historic pottery (1600 CE) from the Northeast consists of the same brownish gray inscribed pottery but with more pronounced collared necks. The Iroquois were responsible for these interesting pieces of pottery.

Some historic pottery was produced by the Catawba, Pamunkey, Coushatta, and Cherokee east of the Mississippi. The Iroquois and Choctaw made pottery prior to the 1900s, and a few Cherokee groups made pottery in the 1900s.

PREHISTORIC POTTERY

The Midwestern United States had a prolific production of

prehistoric pottery that left a clear archaeological trail of pottery pieces to study and collect.

While the Prehistoric American Indians of the Southwest with their advanced culture were busy producing pottery, baskets, stone tools, and other beautiful items, an equally sophisticated American Indian culture was active in the Mississippi River area doing basically the same things including making pottery. The Mississippian Culture Period evolved from the Woodland Period and encompassed a large group of people over a wide area. When De Soto arrived in 1541, the Mississippian Culture was nearing the top of its form; by 1673 when the French explorers Marquette and Joliet arrived, the Mississippian Culture had nearly vanished except for a few Quapaw villages. Disease brought in by De Soto's people and intertribal fighting probably caused the demise of the Mississippian Culture's early people who made a large quantity of pottery consisting of various shapes, sizes, and types.

The Prehistoric Mississippian Indians north of the Arkansas River used crushed shell to temper their clay, while the tribes south of the Arkansas River used crushed bone or pieces of dry clay for temper. Some shell was used in the south after contact with the Europeans.

The women of the Mississippian Culture tribes were the potters (as is true of the Southwest Prehistoric Indians). They used the coil method with decorations made by incising, engraving, puncturing, appliqué, or employing nodes as texture. Decoration was also accomplished with the use of pigments. Polychrome decoration using iron ore as red and kaolin as white was used in the later period of the Mississippian Culture. The black found to have been used in these later Mississippian sites is thought to be derived from a vegetal source. Black was used as a negative decoration in southeastern Missouri and areas eastward.

What is interesting about Mississippian pottery is the various shapes and sizes. Pieces from plain bowls to elaborate effigy pieces were made as both utilitarian and ceremonial vessels. A simple bowl was often transformed into a decorated piece by many methods of surface changes such as incising and puncturing. Sometimes only the rims were decorated; other times it was the whole vessel. The methods of decoration consisted of incising with a pointed tool on wet clay, puncturing (small holes pierced into the wet clay with a tool to make a pattern), engraving (using a sharp tool to scratch a decoration on a fired and finished pottery piece), appliqué (wet clay is applied to a wet clay pot in a linear fashion), and node designs (clay nodes are placed all over a wet clay pot to form a design).

Beautiful water bottles with long necks, bowls with arcade handles, high-side jars, lobed vessels, stirrup vessels, handled double vessels, beaker-shaped pots with handles, and handled bowls are some of the unique shapes the collector will find available to own.

What is more exciting to see, study, and collect is the array of effigy forms made by the Mississippian Culture Indians. Quite common were bowls with added effigy heads at the rim; a wide variety of animal heads as well as human and mystical heads were used. Unique full-bodied effigies of humans, frogs, serpents, dogs, turtles, fish, and birds are fairly prevalent and are beautiful works of art. Most special are the famous human head pots and full-bodied human figures. Prices and availability of such pieces are good.

Quapaw Indian pottery is considered a separate type of Mississippian pottery as it was made by the Quapaw tribe in Arkansas and Mississippi during a later period of time, 1650–1750 CE. To the inexperienced eye, Quapaw pottery looks similar to the later Mississippian Culture pieces. However, it has a unique style of its own that differentiates it from this earlier period.

Beautiful polychrome effigies, long-neck bottles, and unique bowls were made by the Quapaw. Methods of decoration included painting, puncturing, incising, engraving, appliqué, or a combination of these methods. The beautiful polychrome effigies of animals, eccentric forms, and humans are most notable as Quapaw pottery.

To assist you in your study of Mississippian Culture pottery, I have listed below the classifications by period of production.

Incised decoration

Barton: 1200–1600 CE. Incised line-filled triangles or other repeated simple linear patterns used on neck or rims of vessels

Mathews: 1000–1600 CE. Incised lines going around a vessel usually in an undulating design

Mound Placed: 1200–1600 CE. Two or more horizontal incised lines

Ranch: 1400–1600 CE. Curvilinear incised patterns in fish designs

Rhodes: 1450–1600 CE. Closely spaced, trailed with incisions of a scale motif

Wallace: 1400–1700 CE. Broad, shallow, incised with lines on the rims of effigy bowls; Quapaw pottery

Painted decoration

Avenue: 1500–1600 CE. Red on buff swirls and bands; a touch of black is sometimes noticeable.

Carson Red: 1400–1600 CE. Red on buff designs of curvilinear and geometric motifs

Nodena Red & White: 1500–1600 CE. Red and white spiraling swirls

Plain

Bell: 1200–1600 CE. Lustrous gray on shell-tempered pottery

Baytown: 1 BCE–1200 CE. Plain gray

Larto Red: 400–1200 CE. Red slip on clay-tempered pottery;

Old Town Red is classified with shell-tempered pottery.

Neeley's Ferry: 1200–1600 CE. Buff-finished

Punctuated

Campbell: 1400–1600 CE. Vertical lines of small holes

Parkin: 1200–1600 CE. Puncture holes or dash marks all over vessel on shell-tempered pottery

Engraved

Hull: 1400–1600 CE. Engraved inside as well as outside of vessel, consisting of fish scale and concentric arcs

Walls: 1400–1600 CE. Fine linear, shallow engraving, usually using cross-hatching to fill circular bands

Node

Bank Node: 1200–1600 CE. One or two rows of nodes on a vessel

Fortune: 1200–1600 CE. Closely placed nodes of clay covering the whole vessel

Appliqué

Vernon Paul: 1400–1600 CE. Parallel strips about 2 mm high and 1–2 mm apart applied as ridges on the body of the vessel, each being smoothed into the pot

Combination

Combinations of two or more of the above. Decorative techniques are commonly used; an example is a bowl with a Fortune node and Vernon-appliquéd rim.

SOUTHWEST PREHISTORIC POTTERY

The Southwestern United States has produced prehistoric and historic pottery that has tickled the collector's fancy (see map 2). Prehistoric pottery of the Southwest comes in various shapes and sizes from large ollas to tiny miniature effigy pieces. A variety of colors such as polychrome, black, red-on-white, black-on-white, black-on-red, and black-on-yellow were used. Designs from geometric to zoomorphic pictorial bowls were made, and all are available to the collector, museums, and students of archaeology.

The prehistoric pottery artists of the Southwest were excellent creators of unbelievable masterpieces with no two pieces exactly alike, and what is nice for the collector is that there were thousands of pieces made that are available at affordable prices.

True, there are expensive pieces of prehistoric pottery, but for every expensive piece there are hundreds of inexpensive ones. It was through the discovery of ancient artifacts that much of the archaeological study of prehistoric peoples has been accomplished, yet an unknown number of pottery pieces and other prehistoric artifacts remain hidden due to modern day beliefs and laws. Prehistoric items found on public lands are protected by the laws listed in chapter 1 and cannot be excavated or traded. Prehistoric items legally collected from privately owned property are collectible and marketable.

ANASAZI CULTURE PREHISTORIC POTTERY

Listed below are the groups of Anasazi pottery by regions of production, with the earliest made given first (all dates are estimates).

Kayenta group, Northern Arizona

Corrugated: Evenly patterned texture, some with braided handles, gray color; cooking pots, storage vessels, and pitchers

Redware: Orangish red color, smooth surfaces, utilitarian pieces

Painted: Organic paint was used except on Bidahochi where mineral paint was used:

Kana: black-on-white, 700–850 CE

Black Mesa: black-on-white, 875–1150 CE

Tusayan: black-on-red, 850–1125 CE

Tusayan: black-on-white, 1100–1275 CE

Tusayan: polychrome, 1125–1300 CE

Kayenta: polychrome, 1150–1300 CE

Kiet Si: polychrome, 1150–1300 CE

Bidahochi: black-on-white, 1300–1400 CE

Bidahochi: polychrome 1300–1400 CE

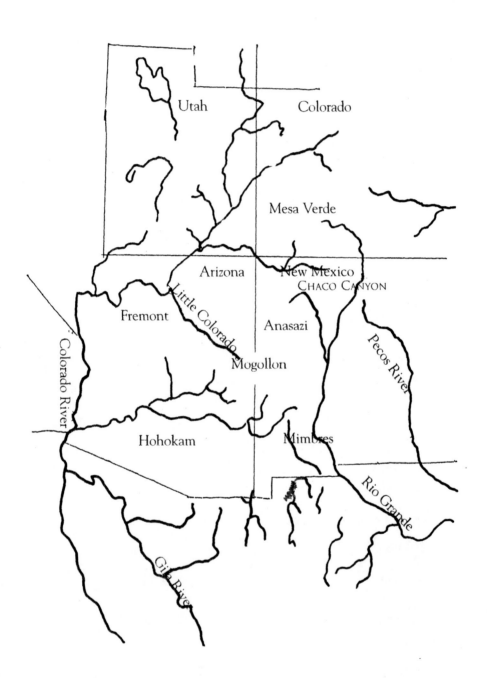

Map 2. Southwest prehistoric pottery - making areas

Jeddito: black-on-orange, 1200–1300 CE

Jeddito: black-on-yellow, 1325–1600 CE

Sikyatki: polychrome, 1400–1650 CE

Mesa Verde Group, Four Corners Area

Corrugated: Beautiful narrow rows of corrugated work was produced on utilitarian pottery. Designs were also scratched on some pieces.

Grayware: Early utilitarian pottery was mainly gray in color and plain.

Painted: Organic as well as mineral paint was used; the mineral paint was black and red.

General observation: Black on white pottery was thick-walled with thick, painted, flat rims. The white slip had a glossy, cracked appearance, and unique to this group were mug-shaped vessels:

Lino: black-on-gray, 600–900 CE

Abajo: red-on-orange, 700–900 CE

La Plata: black-on-orange, 800–950 CE

Mancos: black-on-white, 850–1100 CE

McElmo: black-on-white, 900–1100 CE

Mesa Verde: black-on-white, 1150–1300 CE

Chaco Group, Northeastern New Mexico

Corrugated: Fine small corrugation with some etched-in designs; storage jars, pitchers, and cooking vessels

Redware: Fine polished, red-slipped utilitarian pottery

Painted: Mineral paint was used.

General observation: Later designs show hatched lines inside of dark outlines. Pottery of the Puerco group had a darker gray background:

Kiatuthlanna: black-on-white, 750–850 CE

Red Mesa: black-on-white, 850–950 CE

Puerco: black-on-white, 850–1150 CE

Puerco: black-on-red, 950–1150 CE

Chaco: black-on-white, 950–1150 CE

Cibola Group, North Central Arizona and New Mexico

Corrugated: Note the painted corrugated pottery called *McDonald corrugated*. Simple utilitarian vessels were made as well as fancy etched design pieces.

Redware: Red-slipped utilitarian and some effigy pieces were made.

Painted: Mineral paint was used.

General observation: This group produced more exotic pottery pieces than conservative pieces:

Reserve: black-on-white, 950–1150 CE

Wingate: black-on-red, 950–1150 CE

Tularosa: black-on-white, 1100–1200 CE

St. Johns: black-on-red, 1100–1200 CE

McDonald: polychrome, 1150–1400 CE

Pinedale: polychrome, 1250–1325 CE

Homolovi: polychrome, 1300–1400 CE

Four Mile: polychrome, 1350–1400 CE

Salado Group, North Central Arizona

Corrugated: Fine-to-coarse corrugated utilitarian pieces

Redware: Polished utilitarian and some effigy pieces

Painted: Mineral paint was used.

General observation: Generally better artistic designs:

Snowflake: black-on-white, 975–1100 CE

Roosevelt: black-on-white, 1100–1200 CE

Pinto: polychrome, 1150–1250 CE

Gila: polychrome 1200–1300 CE

Tonto: polychrome, 1300–1400 CE

Miscellaneous Anasazi types

Socorro: black-on-white, 1050–1275 CE

Sagi: black-on-white, 1200–1300 CE

Zuni Glaze: polychrome, 1200–1400 CE

Houck: polychrome, 1200–1250 CE

Querino: polychrome, 1250–1300 CE

San Carlos: red-on-orange tan, 1400–1600 CE

FREMONT CULTURE POTTERY

The Fremont Culture geographically covered most of Utah with the eastern and western boundaries extending slightly into Colorado and Nevada. The period of pottery making extends from 400–1350 CE. The quality of prehistoric Fremont pottery is inferior to the Anasazi, Mogollon, or Hohokam pottery.

Fremont Culture prehistoric pottery is fairly rare to find but is available occasionally. The most unique and beautiful Fremont Culture pottery artifact is the human clay figures. Elaborately decorated with clay appliqué and sometimes painted with red ocher, they are outstanding but very rare. Other types of pottery pieces made were cooking vessels, bowls, and pitchers.

Great Salt Lake Gray: 400–1350 CE. Dark gray surface that is sometimes incised or modeled

Unita Gray: 650–950 CE. Dark gray to light brown color with a smooth surface, sometimes incised, appliquéd, punched, or modeled

Emery Gray: 700–1200 CE. A gray smooth-surfaced pottery, occasionally decorated by appliqué, punching, or incising

Ivie Creek Black-on-White: 700–1200 CE. Smoothed and slipped surface, the slip is creamy white-on-gray; the painted decorations are organic black with geometric designs.

Sevier Gray: 800–1250 CE. Dark gray smooth surface

Snake River Gray: 900–1200 CE. Smooth gray surface, sometimes incised, punched, or appliquéd for design

Snake Valley Black-on-Gray: 900–1200 CE. Smooth light gray surface, no slit, black mineral painted designs

Snake Valley Corrugated: 1100–1200 CE. Gray to reddish gray

Promontory Gray: 1000–1300 CE. Gray, coarsely finished surface, occasionally decorated by appliqué, punching, or incising

HOHOKAM POTTERY

The Hohokam lived in South Central Arizona from 200–1400 CE. They were advanced farmers with an elaborate water canal system to nourish their crops. Their artistic talents are recorded on their very finely designed pottery, cut-and-etched shell jewelry, and numerous other items. Their decorative work seems to have been influenced by their Southern neighbors. Pottery pieces were made either by corrugation, redware, or were painted. The painted pottery is always a dull, maroonish red paint on a tan clay that contains mica and is unslipped.

Corrugated: None, however pottery with etched coils were made.

Redware: Utilitarian pieces including bowls, ollas, jars, and plates were made.

Painted: All Hohokam painted pottery was done with reddish iron oxide applied to a tannish clay pot.

Pioneer: 300 BCE–500 CE. This period was made up of four subclasses—Vahki, Estrella, Sweetwater, and Snaketown. The earliest pottery was Vahki redware. Crude designs appeared in the Estrella stage where red was applied on a gray surface. In the Sweetwater phase some exteriors have simple red line work on a gray surface. Also some grooving of the surface was done during this phase. Red-on-buff was dominate in the Snaketown phase, and better symmetry and art work took place. Life forms, scrolls, bull's-eyes, and simple small elements were introduced during this later phase.

Colonial: 500–900 CE. This period was made up of the Santa Cruz and Gila Butte phases. During the Colonial period distinct forms of pottery became evident, and designs encompassing birds and other animal forms were produced. Designs on pottery showed expanding motifs, interlocking scrolls, and curvilinear patterns. Unique forms such as rectangular pottery boxes and heavily flared rim bowls were made.

Sedentary: 900–1100 CE. Strong patterns and dramatic forms were made during this period, which is also called the Sacation phase. An example is the *Gila Shoulder* ollas.

Classic: 1100–1400 CE. This period covers the end of Hohokam pottery making and the time when they were greatly influenced by their neighbors, the Anasazi. The pottery shows poorer color and the introduction of handles and necks. This is the only period with handled pitchers.

MOGOLLON CULTURE POTTERY

The Mogollon Culture covers the Prehistoric Indians of the mountain regions of what is now Arizona and Southwestern New Mexico from about 300 BCE–1400 CE.

Collectors recognize the Mogollon Culture mainly for its later pottery called Classic Mimbres. Classic Mimbres pottery is the beautiful but expensive black-on-white pieces painted with elaborate animal and geometric designs.

Various archaeologists have established period classifications for the Mogollon Culture based on architectural construction and the movements of sites. Therefore, a classification based purely on types of pottery (the process generally followed in this book) may not be appropriate for the Mogollon. Thus, I have utilized the established period classifications to list the types of pottery from the earliest to latest periods.

There are early examples of red-slipped, brownware, and corrugated pottery. The main forms made were bowls and jars, however nice examples of corrugated Mogollon pottery have been found and collected as well. Brownware, redware, and unpainted pottery can be dated from 200–2000 CE.

> Mogollon 1: Redware and brownware, 300 BCE–400 CE. Unrefined designs, some segmentation of the pot with painted lines evident
>
> Mogollon 2: Red-on-brown, 400–600 CE. More refined painting; used some triangle elements in the designs, red-slipped
>
> Mogollon: Red-on-brown, 600–900 CE. Used hematinic thin slip on the exteriors and interiors of bowls. Painting was divided into four sections with broad, imperfect lines.
>
> Mangus: Black-on-white, 775–1100 CE. Black paint on a white slip with designs framing lines below the rim
>
> Three Circle: Red-on-white, 900–1000 CE. White-slipped, brown paste pottery on interior only. Exterior sometimes slipped brown or red. Out-curving rims prevalent with fairly precise painting. Framing lines below the rim occurred more often at this stage.
>
> Mimbres: Black-on-white, 950–1150 CE: A white-slipped painted surface with black to reddish paint is typical of this phase of Mogollon pottery. Framing near the rims of the pottery is usually done in multiple lines, and the line painting is superior in fineness to the earlier types.

Beautiful geometric designs using curvilinear and various design elements produced the elaborate Mimbres Classic masterpieces. But the pottery most sought after by collectors are the figured bowls with beautifully executed animals, humans, and mystical scenes.

Sometime during the late 1400s and early 1500s the last of what we call Prehistoric Indians disappeared. Most are unaccounted for; some moved to Pueblos and are the predecessors of the historic Pueblo tribes.

HISTORIC POTTERY

For the purpose of understanding the collectibility of historic pottery, I have elected to separate the early historic pieces (1650–1880) from the later historic pieces (1880–1945). Early historic pottery consists of hard-to-find, beautifully constructed pieces. They are very expensive to purchase, when they do become available. The later historic pottery is more available to collect, although prices have gone up considerably.

In the East there is very little historic pottery. The Cherokee of North Carolina and Oklahoma made some urns, vases, bowls, and effigy pieces. Their work is plain or done in a dark finish with an incised design. The Catawba tribe of South Carolina made vases, pitchers, and jars since the 1600s. In Louisiana, the Coushatta made a traditional pottery that is polished black or orange and is decorated with incised marks.

During the early historic period, the Spanish restricted the Pueblo Indians in their use of pottery in daily chores and spiritual rites; therefore, there are fewer of these pieces available for collection.

Later historic pottery (1880–1945) is made up of very traditional ollas and bowls produced in the early period to curio pieces made for the tourist in the later period. Tourist demand influenced pottery making such that less traditional sizes, shapes, and designs came about. These included items such as candlestick holders, human and animal figures, and handled bowls. By 1900, except for ceremonial purposes, pottery was made to sell to the tourist. However, each Pueblo maintained a style of their own.

The Pueblos making early historic pottery are the following:

Acoma. Located in Central New Mexico, also known as Sky City.

Forms: Ollas and bowls

Ollas have straight necks sometimes scalloped at the top. They are widest at the middle and are distinguishable by their thin walls. Bowls are fairly high-walled, roundish, and small to large.

Slip and color: White-slipped, painted black and red

Design: Done in one-to-three horizontal zones from top to bottom. Both ollas and bowls are geometric, curvilinear, and floral; animals were also used.

General observation: Most notable about the Acoma early pottery are the thin walls, a very white slip, and a fully designed surface.

Cochiti. Located near Santa Fe, New Mexico

Forms: Globular ollas, bowls, and canteens

Ollas are round with the necks straight up from the body; occasionally the top of the neck is flared. Bowls have incurvating walls, and canteens are globular with handles. Human figures appeared in the later 1880s.

Slip and color: A creamy tan slip with black-painted designs

Design: Geometric, curvilinear, animal, and symbolic figures were used. Some bowls have designs inside and out. The zone of design is the full working surface.

General observation: Look for a creamy tan slip and a globular appearance done in a black-painted design.

Hopi. The Hopi are located in the Northeastern corner of Arizona at what is known as the First, Second, and Third Mesas. The oldest Hopi group, with ancestors from the Anasazi Sikyatki and Jeddito, are at the Second and Third Mesas. The Hopi Tewa people came from the Rio Grande area of New Mexico about 1700 and occupy the First Mesa with a different language and social order.

Forms: Ollas and bowls

Ollas are round with the widest point 1/2 to 3/4 of the way up. The necks are short, either with outcurving at the lips or straight. Bowls of the 1880s were round with sides coming in near the top and flaring back out a little. A special type of bowl called *Mutton Stew* was made around the early 1880s. This bowl is deep and has a wide flaring rim. At the time of the revival of pottery in the late 1890s by Nampeyo of Hano, a squat olla form developed with a short neck and flat bottom.

Slip and color: There is a unslipped Hopi type called *Walpi* and two slipped types called *Polacca* and *Hano*. Painting on both are polychrome red and black on a yellowish orange slip or base; the underbodies are red. Later red and white slips came about.

Design: Beautiful curved lines to make feathers, fingers, beaks, and comma designs. Also, kachina faces and Zuni-like figures are incorporated into the designs.

General observation: Early Hopi pottery has a cracked, lustrous yellow slip painted in red and black that is easily distinguished. Nampeyo of Hano pieces have hooklike spirals, wide feather designs, and red-filled figures.

Laguna. This Pueblo is located in Central New Mexico.

Forms: Bowls, ollas, and some effigy forms

Bowls curve outward from a round base; the widest diameter is just below the rim. Ollas are globular with the widest diameter midway. They have a curved base with the sides curving outward from the base to midway. The necks on the olla are short and slanting into a rim that can be straight or fluted.

Slip and color: Slip is white similar to the Acoma, and the designs are painted in red, orange, yellow, and dark brown. The base is red-slipped.

Design: The designs cover all of the outside surface and are similar to the Acoma.

General observation: Laguna and Acoma are almost identical, except that Laguna ollas are not as finely finished, although the bowls are equal or better in design.

San Ildefonso. This Pueblo is located just north of Santa Fe, New Mexico, and is the Pueblo of the world-famous potter, Maria Martinez.

> Forms: The potters from this Pueblo made small to very large ollas and bowls. The bowls are fairly shallow, and the widest diameter is midway on the earliest pots, dropping to below the midway point on the later ones.
>
> Slip and color: The early slip used was stone-polished creamy tan. By 1900 the potters changed to a Cochiti slip applied with a rag. The designs were done in black in the early 1880s, and later in black and red. A red-slipped rim was on the older pots; after 1897, black was used. The potters of this Pueblo were also known for making black-on-red pottery between 1880 and 1890.
>
> Design: The design consists of plant forms, solid elements, angular, and curved-lined figures. The zones of design are in two and three horizontal bands; the bands are usually two on the neck area and one covering the body area. Animal figures were sometimes incorporated into the designs after 1905.
>
> General observation: These polychrome and black-on-red pottery pieces are very distinguishable. The black-on-red pottery also has an inside ledge just below the top of the rim, a place for a lid to rest upon.

San Juan. This Pueblo is just north of Santa Fe, New Mexico, near the Santa Clara Pueblo.

> Forms: This Pueblo made large storage ollas with large mouths and short necks. The bowls are high-walled, incurving at top to a wide rim on one type and a short-lipped rim on another. The widest point on the ollas and bowls is midway.
>
> Slip and color: San Juan pottery is burnished blackware and redware. The upper two-thirds of each pot show a slip, giving the redware a tan bottom and the blackware a gray bottom.
>
> Design: None

General observation: San Juan pottery is blackish or reddish with only two-thirds of the piece slipped.

Santa Ana. This Pueblo is located near Santa Fe, New Mexico.

Forms: This Pueblo made ollas and bowls. The ollas are globular with short necks and a wide opening; medium to fairly large ollas were made.

Slip and color: The slip used is cream, and the designs are painted with red or black.

Design: The design is in a wide zone around the pot with a band of design on the short neck of the olla. The design itself is geometric and large, curved-shaped with straight lines, and blocky-looking figures; the figures are painted inside with red and outlined in black. Black elements will also be in the pot.

General observation: These pots are globular-looking, distinguished by the fat, block-shaped red designs outlined in black on a dull, dirty-looking cream slip.

Santa Clara. This Pueblo is located just north of Santa Fe, New Mexico.

Forms: Bowls, long-neck ollas, wedding vases, and small to medium pieces were made. Ollas are globular with tall necks or short necks. The tall-neck olla has a prominent shoulder with an outward curve at the angle at the base of the neck. Bowls can be curved at the top to form a seed jar look. Small bowls can have walls that are incurving, straight, and/or outward.

Slip and color: These older Santa Clara pots are fired black.

Design: Decoration is accomplished by indentions; the *Bear Paw* indention is indicative of Santa Clara pottery.

General observation: The early Santa Clara pottery has a black polished finish with indented designs. The Wedding Vase and shouldered neck black pottery are distinguishable as Santa Clara pottery.

Santo Domingo. This old Pueblo is just south of Santa Fe and north of Albuquerque, New Mexico.

Forms: Globular ollas and bowls. Ollas have distinct necks, shoulders, and flared rims, with the widest diameter midway between the base and rim. Ollas can be medium to large. Bowls consist of small to large dough bowls, small chili bowls, and large storage high-walled bowls. The rims of the bowls can be flared or straight.

Slip and color: Red is the underbody, and the base slip is a tan cream color. Black painted geometric elements in wide horizontal bands are used to decorate.

Design: On ollas and large storage jars, usually two horizontal zones of designs were used; one covered the bulk of the body, the other the neck. Bowls usually have one large horizontal band of repeated geometric elements, however each element can differ.

General observation: Santo Domingo historic bowls have a distinct appearance of their own. They are thick-walled with black heavy designs on a cream outer slip over a reddish underbody. The only other Pueblo pottery similar to Santo Domingo is Cochiti, and one can tell it from Santo Domingo by its more curvilinear designs and thinner walls.

Tesuque. A small Pueblo in the cluster of Pueblos near Santa Fe, New Mexico

Forms: All

Slip and color: Cream-colored slip and black design paint is most common. Some polychromes were done by the addition of red.

Design: The design work is masterfully executed. Some characteristic designs are fingerlike feathers, diagonally hatched strips, and radiating feather clusters.

General observation: Tesuque pottery is very distinguishable, once one has learned about it. It has a strong execution of sensitive design work.

Zia. This small Pueblo is located near Santa Fe, New Mexico.

Forms: Ollas and bowls make up the main forms that the Zia historically made. Ollas are globular with a wide opening neck. The neck appears to slant in from the body to the rim. It really is not a distinct neck. The body of the olla is widest at the middle, gracefully outcurving from the shoulder to the midpoint then forming a slight incurve as it meets the base. Bowls can be very deep when larger. The upper rim area incurvates to form a bowl with the widest diameter close to the upper area. Smaller bowls were also made, but the rim is outcurved and the walls slant a little outward.

Slip and color: The slip is a dullish gray, cream color over a primary red undercoat. The design colors are reddish orange and black.

Design: The ollas have wide double meandering bands encircling the piece up on the shoulder to down near the base. These meandering bands usually go over geometric, plant, and bird figures in the center of the pot. The design can cover from rim to near the base, and some ollas have a zone of design around the neck rim area. Designs on bowls consist of differing geometric elements with a broad band in the upper portion of the bowl. Usually a double line outlines the zone of the design.

General observation: The decorative motif is very distinctive on Zia pottery; usually on ollas you will have the broad meandering zones of design with a bird figure.

Zuni. This unique Pueblo is about 20 miles from Gallup, New Mexico.

Forms: The Zuni historic pottery includes medium to large ollas, small and large bowls, kiva bowls, effigy figures, and canteens. Ollas have a distinct neck which takes up to 25 percent of the olla. The widest diameter of the olla is near the top of the body. The olla curves inward from the shoulder to the base. Bowls are usually shallow and can have a flat or round base. All bowls curve up from the base, ending in a rim that can be slightly outslanted. Canteens are barrel-shaped, multiglobed, triangular-shaped, and globular. Canteens are generally moderate to small in size and with or without handles.

Slip and color: The underbody is dark brown; the final slip over the brown underbody is creamy white. The designs are painted prior to firing in dark brown and reddish brown.

Design: Ollas have elaborate designs of combinations of elements in horizontal and vertical zones. In the zones are painted scrolls, rosettes, birds, deer, red heart lines, serrated lines, and fine lines. Design zones include a zone around the neck and one or more around the body with designs from the rim to near the base. Bowls can be painted inside and out. Bowls' interior designs are the same as those described for ollas. The exterior design consists of serrated diagonal elements made up of dark triangles on a slanted line with hooked elements ending in an elongated triangle. Designs on kiva bowls are the same as on ollas but also include tadpoles, frogs, dragonflies, and serpents. Canteens have the same designs as ollas and kiva bowls.

General observation: Zuni pottery is very distinct and once you have become familiar with a few pieces you will be able to identify it easily. The distinct colors of a brown undercoating with creamy gray slip and dark reddish brown painted figures of deer, rosettes, and such will be easy to distinguish.

POSTHISTORIC AMERICAN INDIAN POTTERY

Pottery made after 1900 is generally referred to as contemporary pottery. Since this covers 96 years of pottery making, and since the first 45 years marked an interesting era of famous Indian potters, for simplicity and better understanding I have divided this long period of time into posthistoric pottery (1900–1945) and contemporary pottery (1945 to present). Discussion will be confined to posthistoric pottery.

The posthistoric period produced large quantities of Southwest collectible

Indian pottery. Prices for pottery of the unsigned and less-known artists of this period are still bargains.

Unique to Southwest Indian pottery is that, beginning with the posthistoric period, the maker of the piece usually signed the bottom of the pot. Thus, collectors could identify not only which Pueblo the piece came from but also the artist. Each potter has an individual style which has led to collectors seeking out the pieces of specific artists.

During the posthistoric period the Southwest Indians made pottery primarily for resale, except for a few ceremonial pieces.

One of the most famous of all Southwest potters, Maria Martinez from Santo Domingo, worked on pottery from about 1887 when she was 7 years old until the 1960s when she worked with her son, Popovi Da. Prior to 1919, Maria had mastered the art of making large, hard-fired vessels with thin walls, beautiful shapes, and beautifully smoothed surfaces. The great designs were a creation of her husband, Julian. With the help of Julian, in 1919 Maria developed a method to make black matte on polished blackware.

The popularity for collecting Maria's pottery is now worldwide. Thanks to her prolificness, thousands of "Maria pieces" are available to collect. The beauty of her finished black matte on black pottery work is unsurpassed due to the great polish work and expert designs.

Lucy Lewis and Marie Z. Chino of the Acoma Pueblo revived the prehistoric pottery design motif. These women, with the help of Jessie Garcia, started making pottery in the 1920s. This set a trend in the new designs that flourished during the 1950s. Lucy Lewis introduced the Mimbres and Hohokam prehistoric designs into Acoma pottery. Today, Lucy Lewis pottery is aggressively collected, and prices have advanced sharply since her death.

At Santa Clara Pueblo, Margaret Tafoya mastered the technique of making large incised black matte pottery. Margaret's pottery is extremely collectible and very expensive.

Listed below are the Southwest Pueblos with a brief description of the pottery made by them after 1900. Collectibility and the general quality of pieces are also noted.

Acoma

Color and design: This pottery has a white slip (kaolin) with black-on-white, white-on-black, and polychrome (black, orange, and black-on-white) colors. The designs are distinguishable as fine-line black-on-white, birds, deer, and flowers in polychrome. The design usually covers the entire piece.

Forms: Bowls, ollas, canteens, jars, vases, owls, turtles, and miniatures.

Collectibility: There is good availability and affordability.

Quality: Acoma patterns are known for their full but strong design.

Cochiti

Color and design: The Cochiti potter uses the traditional cream-colored slip with black and red design work. Designs are simple geometric and animals. They often used rain symbols and curvilinear leaflike motifs.

Forms: Bowls, ollas, jars, canteen, animal and human effigies, as well as storytellers.

Collectibility: Although not as plentiful as some other Pueblo pottery, Cochiti pottery is quite available and generally inexpensive.

Quality: Generally very good.

Hopi

Color and design: The pottery of the Hopi consists of black-on-red, black-on-white, black- and red-on-tan, or plain white and plain red. The slips are red, white, and tan. Designs done in black and red are curvilinear lines and stylized feathers and birds.

Forms: Bowls, ollas, tall cylinders, wedding vases, animal figures, canteens, and squat ollas and bowls.

Collectibility: There is an excellent supply of pottery from the 1920s through the 1940s. Prices range from inexpensive to very expensive for the better and rarer pieces.

Quality: Generally the quality is good except for some smeared paint on the early 1900s pieces. The walls are usually thick and strong.

Isleta

Color and design: Small polychrome pottery pieces were made just after 1900. Reddish orange and black on a white slip are the colors used. The designs are simple geometric lines and reddish dots.

Forms: Small bowls, with or without handles, wedding vases, and ollas.

Collectibility: Isleta pieces commonly show up, but most collectors pass them by as too touristlike or unidentifiable. If collectors understood the scarcity of this pottery, they would gobble them up. Prices are inexpensive.

Quality: The workmanship is good on the older pieces.

Laguna

Color and design: The use of a white slip is prevalent with reddish orange and black for polychrome pieces and black-on-white for other pottery.

Forms: Bowls, canteens, jars, vases, ollas, and some figures were made.

Collectibility: Older pottery from Laguna is heavily sought after.

Quality: Very good.

Maricopa

Color and design: The Maricopa make a reddish maroon pot and a black-on-white pot. The designs are painted or appliquéd.

Forms: Long-necked vases, bowls, figurines, pitchers, wedding vases, and bowls with handles.

Collectibility: The finer pieces are very collectible, and there are small, inexpensive pieces on the market for the beginner collector.

Quality: Generally good, however pottery that has been damp will show peeling of the paint.

Mojave

Color and design: The background is an unslipped tan, and the designs are painted in red. Some of the pottery forms have strings of beadwork added for decoration.

Forms: Human effigies, bowls, pitchers, cups, and handled jars.

Collectibility: These are very desirable, and the prices have remained fairly inexpensive.

Quality: The workmanship is good and has a modern appeal.

Navajo

Color and design: Navajo pottery has a reddish brown color due to it being coated with piñon pine resin prior to firing. Designs are applied with appliqué.

Forms: Navajo pottery is usually under 12 inches high. It is pear-shaped and can be a jar, wedding vase, or drum-shaped piece. Very early pieces were actually used as drums.

Collectibility: Until the 1920s most of the Navajo pottery was made for their own use. Since then potters are making a good quantity of quality pieces for sale with reasonable prices.

Quality: Quality is good.

San Ildefonso

Color and design: San Ildefonso is best known for its black matte pottery, however some polychrome pieces were made. The polychrome is a cream-colored slip with black and reddish orange designs. Designs consist of the water serpent, feathers, geometric elements, and natural symbols.

Forms: Ollas, plates, bowls, seed jars, wedding vases and effigies.

Collectibility: Most San Ildefonso pottery is highly collectible. Prices can be high, but there is plenty available.

Quality: These pottery pieces are excellent.

Santa Ana

Color and design: Redware and polychrome make up the two types of pottery made. The polychrome has a cream slip with red and black painted designs of curved and straight lines and elements. Designs of lightning, rainbows, and clouds are also incorporated into the decoration of the pottery.

Forms: Ollas, bowls, effigies, and handled bowls

Collectibility: Availability is very low and prices can be high.

Quality: The polychrome pots are beautiful while the redware is not as sought after.

Santa Clara

Color and design: This very active pottery group produces polychrome, polished blackware, and polished redware. They decorate their pottery by painting. The polychrome pieces can be white or tan background with red, orange, and black designs.

Forms: Ollas, miniatures, seed bowls, dishes, and bowls

Collectibility: There are hundreds of beautiful, excellent quality pottery pieces available in a good price range.

Quality: The art work on this pottery is excellent.

Santo Domingo

Color and design: The Santo Domingo potters make a traditional black-on-buff and black-on-red with a red base. Pottery designs are repeated geometric elements arranged in panels and bands. Birds, flowers, and animal figures are commonly used, and the spirit break appears in nearly all pieces.

Forms: Large bowls, ollas, canteens, handled bowls, dough bowls, chili bowls, and pitchers

Collectibility: There are a sufficient amount of older pieces available and at good prices.

Quality: The quality is good. Usually Santo Domingo pottery is thick-walled with very traditional designs.

Tesuque

Color and design: A few polychrome pottery pieces have been made, and some black-on-red has been produced, but generally Tesuque is known for its *Rain Gods*, painted traditionally prior to 1930 and with bright poster paints thereafter. These Rain Gods were made for the tourist and not for use by the Pueblo.

Forms: Effigies, bowls, ollas, vases, and handled bowls

Collectibility: The older pieces are nice and very hard to find. Rain Gods are seen in many places but are not highly desired by serious collectors.

Quality: The older, traditionally made pieces are good. The later poster-painted pieces usually lose their paint.

Zia

Color and design: The Zia made a beautiful polychrome that has a creamy white slip with black-, red-, and orange-painted designs. These pots have a red, unfinished base that is separated from the painted design area by a double band encircling the pot. Designs consist of birds, deer, and floral motifs. Some pieces have repeated geometric designs only. Large swirled, doubled bands are quite often used to engulf the main design.

Forms: Ollas, bowls, dough bowls, jars, seed jars, canteens, pitchers, and effigies

Collectibility: Zia pottery is highly collectible.

Quality: The quality of this Pueblo pottery is excellent.

Zuni

Color and design: The Zuni made a very traditional style of pottery. Their polychrome pieces consist of a grayish white slip decorated with dark brown and orangish red-painted designs. The base and rim of the pot are painted in dark brown.

Forms: Ollas, kiva bowls, frogs, owls, and bowls. Bowls and ollas with appliquéd pottery frogs are very collectible.

Collectibility: The Zuni were very prolific makers of historic pottery, but not prolific posthistoric potters. So pottery from this time period is hard to find and the prices can be high.

Quality: Zuni pottery is of excellent quality.

POTTERY-MAKING TECHNIQUES

Since prehistoric times American Indian potters have used the coil method to make pottery. Traditional American Indian pottery is never made on a potter's wheel. The construction of pottery consists of:

1. gathering the clay and temper
2. cleaning the clay
3. mixing the clay, temper, and water
4. working the clay to the proper texture
5. forming the coils and molding a start
6. building the walls from the start at the bottom by adding coils

7. smoothing the walls inside and out
8. thinning the walls
9. adding a slip to the pottery
10. polishing the piece while still wet
11. drying the pottery
12. decorating the pottery
13. firing the pottery

Firing is done outdoors with a fire 1500°F for up to 3 hours. Blackware is produced when the fire is smothered with animal dung to produce a carbon that makes the pottery black. Regular firing with no reduction is called oxidation firing, and it produces redware and lighter-colored pottery.

COLLECTING, MARKETING, AND CARING FOR YOUR POTTERY

Locating collectible American Indian pottery is basically pretty easy. Finding rare top-of-the-line pieces is difficult but fun. Market conditions are strong but there is good availability. Prehistoric pottery has suffered some loss of collector interest due to the problems with illegal digging vs. legal pottery.

Caring for the collection you build is very important. You are collecting a breakable, easily chipped commodity. Proper displaying and storage is very important. Open shelving or closed cabinets that are wide enough to allow plenty of room for the pottery pieces is needed. On shelves or in cabinets, always allow at least 2 inches of space between pottery pieces to prevent them from hitting together.

If in an earthquake-prone area, try to secure the pottery with soft clay or wax (e.g., Tacky Wax) on the bottom, and be sure the cabinet or shelves will not fall over easily. Light and temperature do not have much effect on pottery, so your displaying is made easier in that respect. Small hands and pets can be detrimental to pottery, so place pieces out of their reach. Storage should be done with each piece wrapped separately, then put into strong boxes with padding placed between each piece. Do not stack the boxes too high on top of each other. In handling pottery, take only one piece at a time in two hands and be sure you have a good hold.

Cleaning pottery is simple. Dusting may be all that is needed, or use a damp cloth with water to remove grime. If grime is deep-encrusted, as on some prehistoric pottery, use warm water with a dry soap bleach (like Biz). Soak overnight and rewash until clean, then rinse in clean water.

Keep records of your pottery collectibles as recommended for baskets.

Can pottery be repaired? Yes, it can. Most prehistoric pottery is restored. The value of prehistoric pottery is changed only slightly if repaired, unless extensive work is done. Historic pottery loses considerable value if broken and restored. However, there are excellent restorers for all types of pottery.

REPRODUCTIONS

Yes, there are a few reproductions in pottery. Until recently, there were little or no reproductions in prehistoric pottery. Now a few pieces occasionally pop up. In the Midwest there are a number of examples of fake Quapaw pottery that have been found. In other cases, it has been discovered that a rebuilt pot (especially Mimbres pottery) contained only a small percentage of an authentic prehistoric pot. Also, complete repainting of pottery is becoming more prevalent. This greatly reduces the resale value of the pot.

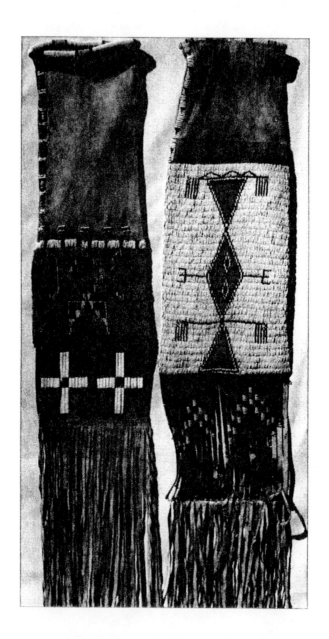

Sioux pipe bags

4

QUILLWORK, BEADWORK, AND OTHER
AMERICAN INDIAN DECORATED
COLLECTIBLES

HISTORY

Archeological finds indicate that since earliest times American Indians have had a keen interest in decorating items of everyday use.

The first types of decoration used were seed, stones, shells, wood, painted hides, horn, and claws. The archaeologist however, cannot pinpoint the first usage of porcupine or bird quillwork by the American Indian. Quillworking tools and pieces of quillwork have been dated to 500 CE. This puts quillwork decoration well into the prehistoric period.

Quillwork is distinctly an American Indian art form, even though the American Indians who were producing these pieces did not consider it an art. The areas of usage extended from Alaska across to Nova Scotia and included the Plains, the Rocky Mountains, and the Great Lakes regions. True, some American Indians did not have access to porcupines from which to collect quills, but they traded with those tribes who were able to obtain quill. Quills, therefore, became a medium of exchange.

QUILLWORK, MATERIALS, AND TECHNIQUES

Prior to their artful application, quills must be prepared. This involves harvesting the quills from the porcupine. Usually, the animal was killed as the meat was considered a delicacy. However, there was another method which involved throwing a skin over the porcupine. This caused the porcupine to shoot its quills into the hide for later retrieval. The quills were then plucked and sorted by size. The next step, performed by the women of the tribe, was to dye the quills. This was achieved by boiling the quills with a vegetable matter for color and a mordant to fix the color. Natural vegetable dyes were replaced with synthetic dyes in the late 1800s. The natural vegetable dyes produced yellow, green, red, and black colors, while synthetic dyes were a more vibrant color of red, blue, green, yellow, purple, and black.

The tools needed to do quillwork consisted of an awl, a pouch to hold the quills, bone engravers, knives, and quill flatteners. American Indian women prepared hides for quilling by marking the designs they wanted to apply with a bone or a stone engraver. Sinew was used to apply the quills until cotton thread became available in the late 1800s. Prior to application, the quills were soaked either in warm water or in the mouths of the women who were doing the quillwork. After softening, the quills were flattened by pulling them between the teeth or fingernails; in some cases the quills had to be pounded to soften them.

The four techniques of quill application are wrapping, plaiting, sewing, and weaving. Wrapping consists of wrapping a dried quill around a narrow object such as hair, hide strips, sinew threads, or vegetable fibers. Wrapping is the simplest form of quilling and consists of tucking the quill under itself and then wrapping it around the narrow object as many times as possible. A new quill is then added by twisting its end with the tip of the previous quill with a half turn. Designs are accomplished by introducing a different colored quill.

In plaiting, each quill is worked around two strips of thread held tight between a small stick in the earth and the quill worker's hands. A spreader (a stick several inches wide) is used to keep the threads separated while working. Each quill is passed over the right thread and under the left thread, then over the left and under the right thread. This is continued by adding new quills until a long narrow braid of quill work is completed.

Plaiting can be done with one or two quills. One-quill plaiting results in two series of tall, opposing triangles and in two rounded forms if pulled tight.

Two-quill plaiting develops into a series of small diamonds down the center of the work. Using two colors makes a beautiful diamond pattern design. The finished product is then applied to an object or backing. A good example is the quill work normally seen on old pipe stems. One- and two-quill plaiting is also often seen on horn spoon handles.

In the sewing technique, the prepared quills are sewn onto the surface to be decorated with a thread or fiber. The flattened quills are folded over and under the threads while being attached to a hide at the same time. This method was used by most of the Plains tribes.

With the development of the bow loom, woven quillwork was produced. A warp of fiber is stretched to each end of the bow and is kept separate from similar fibers by a piece of bark through which all the fibers go. The quills are woven between the various threads producing a fairly wide strip of beautiful quillwork that can be applied to a backing or garment. Woven quillwork results in fine geometric designs and a very fine weave (diagram 5).

TYPES OF QUILLWORK

Quillwork is aggressively collected when available. A limited amount of antique quill pieces reach the market. Bird quillwork is very rare and hard to find.

Most tribes stopped producing quilled pieces after the emergence of the glass bead. The Sioux and the Crow tribes, however, never totally discontinued quillwork. The time periods involved with beadwork and quillwork are:

> Pre-reservation
> Post-reservation
> Reservation
> Contemporary

Pre-reservation covers the period prior to 1880 when American Indians lived on open lands. The reservation period encompasses 1880 until 1910–1920, post-reservation includes the years 1920–1940, and contemporary spans everything from 1940 to the present.

Quill Plating

Quill Plating

Quill Sewing

One Thread, One Quill Sewing

*Two Examples of Two Thread, One Quill,
Straight Sewing*

Two Thread, One Quill Diagonal Sewing

Two Thread, One Quill Crossed Sewing

*Two Quill Plaiting or Sewing, Creating
Small Diamonds Down Center*

Multiple Plaiting Quill

Diagram 5. Quillwork techniques

BEADING

By the mid–1600s glass beads obtained in trade had largely supplanted the traditional shell bead both as jewelry and as currency, so that after hundreds of years of using quills to decorate their belongings, the American Indians switched to glass beads known as pony beads. These white, blue, black, red, and translucent red beads were about 3 mm in size. The pony bead got its name because the traders packed in the beads on ponies. The first usage of beads by American Indians was mainly to trim quill pieces. As the 1840s approached a greater supply became available, and American Indians began to cover larger areas of their work with beads.

American Indians did beadwork in the Great Lakes, Northeast, Northwest, Plains, Prairie, Southeast, Southwest, West, Alaska, and Canada. To aid your understanding of the extent of tribal beadwork, refer to map 3 which shows the tribes and their locations in North America.

Beads were certainly easier to apply than quills. Unlike the quills, they required no preliminary preparation. Beads also allowed wider use of colors and were very durable. Pieces done with pony beads are very hard to find or collect today. Museums are the best places to view works decorated with pony beads, as most pieces are in museums or in a few advanced collectors' collections.

The next change in materials used by American Indians to decorate their belongings came in the 1840–1850s with the introduction of a smaller glass bead called the *seed bead*. The earlier seeds beads were made in Europe and China, while the later ones came from Czechoslovakia and Japan. Venetian beads measured about 1.5 to 3 mm and can be distinguished from today's glass beads by their irregular shape and size. Seed beads came in many colors and gave the American Indian a palette of richly colored beads with which to work. Faceted and metallic beads were also introduced about this time.

When looking at beadwork for collecting, always magnify the piece to determine the type of seed bead. This will aid you in fixing the time period and thus the approximate age of the piece being examined, assuming it was put together near the time the beads were given to the Native Americans.

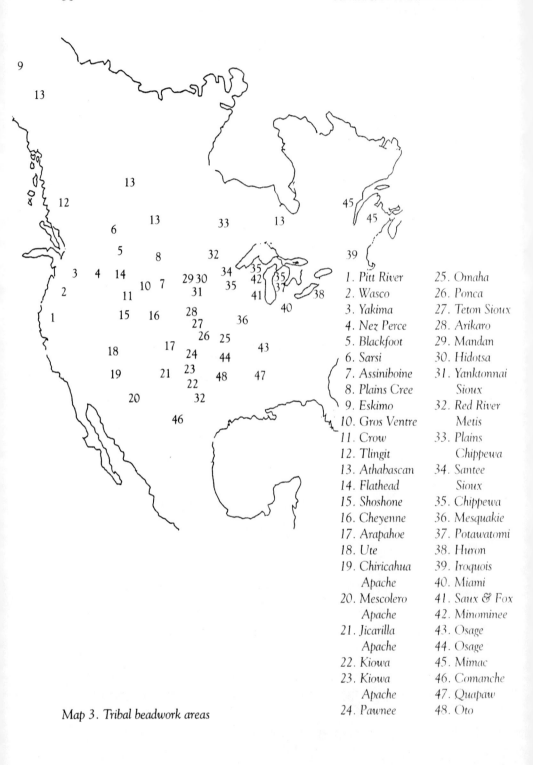

1. Pitt River
2. Wasco
3. Yakima
4. Nez Perce
5. Blackfoot
6. Sarsi
7. Assiniboine
8. Plains Cree
9. Eskimo
10. Gros Ventre
11. Crow
12. Tlingit
13. Athabascan
14. Flathead
15. Shoshone
16. Cheyenne
17. Arapahoe
18. Ute
19. Chiricahua
    Apache
20. Mescolero
    Apache
21. Jicarilla
    Apache
22. Kiowa
23. Kiowa
    Apache
24. Pawnee

25. Omaha
26. Ponca
27. Teton Sioux
28. Arikaro
29. Mandan
30. Hidotsa
31. Yanktonnai
    Sioux
32. Red River
    Metis
33. Plains
    Chippewa
34. Santee
    Sioux
35. Chippewa
36. Mesquakie
37. Potawatomi
38. Huron
39. Iroquois
40. Miami
41. Saux & Fox
42. Minominee
43. Osage
44. Osage
45. Mimac
46. Comanche
47. Quapaw
48. Oto

Map 3. Tribal beadwork areas

From 1900 to 1930 beads became almost uniform in size and a little larger overall and sometimes (as in the case of Czechoslovakian beads) lacked the luster of the older beads. Beads purchased today, however, are perfect in size and shape and are Japanese or newer European beads. Some newer beads show equatorial bands.

Strands of sinew were used to apply the beads to hide or trade cloth, but as cotton thread became available it was more commonly used.

Bead application (stitching)

There are six methods used by American Indians to apply beads to hide or cloth. They are lazy stitch, overlay stitch, crow stitch, netted gourd stitch, netted brick stitch, and loom weaving. The latter was done separately and then sewn onto a backing.

Certain tribes always used the same method of bead application. Therefore, one can figure out which group of American Indians made the pieces by determining the method of application. One still needs to use design, bead color, and other clues to pinpoint it to a specific tribe.

The Central Plains tribes—Sioux, Cheyenne, and Arapaho—were the main tribes who used lazy stitch. The lazy stitch method consists of eight to ten beads strung on a thread to form a row that is sewn down to the backing only at the ends. By doing parallel rows a large area could be covered fairly fast, thus the name, *lazy stitch*. The Cheyenne lazy stitch can be distinguished from the work of other tribes by observing the way that the rows of beads line up evenly and flat on the whole surface. This is caused by looping the thread at the end of each row around the last bead in the previous row and pulling the row tight.

The overlay stitch (also called the spot stitch) method involves a string of beads laid down in a straight or curved line, then every first to third bead is sewn onto the backing with a second thread. This produces a very solidly attached piece of beadwork when repeated hundreds of times. The Northern Plains tribes such as the Blackfoot, Gros Ventre, Sarsi, Plains Cree, and Assiniboine used this method.

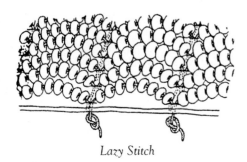

Lazy Stitch

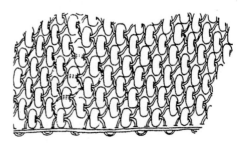

Netted Gourd Stitch

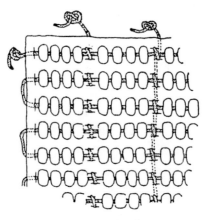

Crow Stitch

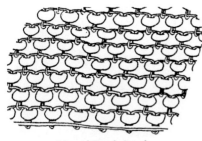

Netted Brick Stitch

Overlay or Spot Stitch

Diagram 6. Beadwork techniques

The crow stitch is similar to the lazy stitch but is secured to the backing every fourth or fifth bead with another thread. It was used by the Crow tribe.

The Comanche and Kiowa of the Southern Plains tribes used what is called the netted stitch. This encompasses both gourd and brick stitching. Please refer to diagram 6 on bead application to see how it is done.

Although Southern Plains tribes preferred not to cover large areas with beads, they liked to bead edges and to include strips of beads on hide cloth. One can usually distinguish pieces decorated by Southern Plains tribes due to the elaborate fringes, painted areas, and the use of tin cones. They also liked small-sized beads and cut-glass beads.

The Great Lakes tribes were trading for beads with the fur traders in the 1700s. In the early 1800s smaller beads became available for the beading of clothing and other items. The overlay stitch was one of their main methods of beading, but the Great Lakes tribes were actually prolific producers of loom beading. Loom beading utilizes a loom, stretching warp threads as the base for the piece while the weft threads carry the beads. There are various types of looms. Examples of beautiful loom work are the panels and straps on the bandolier bags from the Great Lakes.

BEADWORK DESIGNS

Early beadwork, like early quillwork, had designs that were simple. Squares, triangles, bars, and diamond shapes were done alone or in a series until about 1860 when designs became more elaborate, and each tribe developed its own traditional designs. By 1890 the use of elaborate designs by the Plains tribes was common; expanded appendage designs by the Sioux tribe is a good example.

The two main types of beadwork designs are floral and geometric. Zoomorphic figures were occasionally done and are very collectible.

Floral designs originated in the Woodlands Great Lakes area and moved westward: The Minnesota Santee Sioux moved west to Nebraska in 1863, the Plains Cree and Ojibwa moved to the Northern Plains in 1850–1900, and the Great Lakes tribes moved into Kansas and Nebraska around 1860. All these tribes were doing floral beadwork before moving westward.

It is difficult to distinguish the work of each tribe who produced floral beadwork, but there are subtle clues. Geometric designs were easier to do and are representative of the Northern Plains Indians by the Blackfoot, Assiniboine, Gros Ventre, Sioux, Plains Cree, and Sarsi. The Central Plains tribes of the Cheyenne, Sioux, and Arapaho also produced beautiful geometric patterns.

Most of the loom beadwork designs are geometric, although stylized floral loom work is fairly common. Some beautiful zoomorphic work will occasionally show up in loom form.

ITEMS QUILLED OR BEADED

The American Indians decorated almost all of their personal items; very seldom can you find items without any decoration. When the American Indians decorated their possessions or items for trade, they put their spirit into them.

American Indians were on the reservations beginning about 1890, and they had more time on their hands; thus they were prolific producers of beadwork and other items. Most of the beaded and quilled pieces you will find today were made during the Reservation period. This was a period of extreme poverty for the tribes and anything that could be made for sale to the tourist became a necessity: bottles, baby bibs, metal utensils, doctor's bags, suitcases, and just about anything stationary was beaded. It's been said that if a tourist had stood still long enough, the American Indian would have beaded him.

Personal clothing items were also decorated including vests, coats, pants, war shirts, moccasins, leggings, gauntlets (gloves), dresses, and hats. Old American Indian wearing apparel is very collectible as are the later-made pieces.

Beautiful ornamental pieces including necklaces, arm bands, blanket strips, cuffs, rosettes, hair drops, breastplates, and head bands were decorated with beadwork and quills.

Carrying bags and containers were almost always decorated. Beautiful *possible bags* (Indian suitcases), medicine bags, scissor bags, watch bags, peace medal bags, pouches, ration bags, pipe bags, strike-a-lites (fire starting equipment), paint bags, and awl cases are highly collectible and available to own.

The American Indians thought the world of their children, as they still do today, and made beaded and, sometimes, quilled balls, dolls, cradles, bonnets, amulets (fetishes), and toys for them. Another important part of the American Indian's life on the Plains was the horse. So they decorated their horses with beaded and quilled saddles, reins, martingales, cruppers (tail decorations), horse blankets, blinders, and quirts (whips).

American Indian weaponry and ceremonial gear was a necessity in times of war and ceremonial life. Weaponry was both plain and decorated. Examples of these collectibles are knives and knife sheaths, guns and gun cases, pistol cases, lances, spears, pipe stems, rattles, quivers and bow cases, tomahawks, clubs, and dance sticks.

The Iroquois made beaded boots, hearts, birds, boxes, pillows, and other objects to sell at Niagara Falls in the late 1800s through the early 1900s. Today these items are called *whimsies*. Articles have been written about their collectibility, and many authors seek out whimsies. They are very well crafted and are still inexpensive.

FINDING COLLECTIBLE BEADWORK AND QUILLWORK

There are many collectors of decorated American Indian pieces, however the supply of antique beadwork and quillwork is becoming hard to find. Like any collectible field, there are beginner, intermediate, and advanced collectors ready to acquire what they like. Usually collectors will specialize in one type of beadwork or quillwork. For example, collectors may specialize in one tribe (all Cheyenne, Sioux, etc.), or only in beadwork or quillwork. Some collectors acquire it all but specialize in a certain quality.

Finding such items is half the fun of collecting. It spices up our lives as we seek out the pieces we enjoy. Although the antique items are getting harder to locate, they are available.

Dealers who carry a wide selection of old beadwork and guarantee quality and authenticity are among the best sources because:

1. You can get a guarantee from the dealer that the piece is genuine.
2. Dealers' prices are very competitive and sometimes negotiable.
3. Dealers usually can locate the hard-to-get pieces.
4. Dealers are usually willing to give you information not available from other places.

Every collector should find one or two dealers he or she can trust, because these dealers can work for the collector and provide valuable information that is not available elsewhere. True, there are a few dealers who are unwilling to cooperate with collectors regarding guarantees, price, and information, but collectors should not work with these dealers.

Another good supply are auctions. There are more and more auctions for American Indian items. Again, you should be very selective of the auctions from which you buy. The main thing to do at any auction is to preview carefully the items or have somebody do it for you. Some auctions sell items from old collections, while other auctions are dumping grounds for items that buyers have gotten stuck with themselves.

You cannot get a guarantee of quality or authenticity from an auction. In fact, every auction house, under its list of "conditions of sale," specifies that it has done its best to catalog the items correctly, but that it cannot guarantee the correctness of description, tribal designation, age, repairs, restoration, materials, condition, or defects. All items are sold "as is."

Knowing other collectors and buying and trading with them is a good source for beadwork and quillwork. Also, estate sales, yard sales, antique stores, antique shows, Indian shows, and American Indian art galleries are all places where you may find what you are looking for.

Annually, there are three or four good quality antique and contemporary Indian shows. Exhibitors at numerous contemporary American Indian shows are sellers of new items, but you can often find dealers in fine old American Indian antiques at these shows also.

BUYING QUALITY AND AUTHENTICITY

Purchase the best beadwork and quillwork that you can afford. High quality and rare pieces escalate in price the fastest and are the easiest to sell. However, because not everyone can afford the best, you should buy authentic pieces with the best craftsmanship possible.

Quality in beadwork and quillwork is based on the following:

authenticity	rareness
fineness of craftsmanship	excellence of condition

Try to pay market price or less for the beadwork or quillwork you acquire, as overpaying only eats up your initial appreciation and makes reselling more difficult later on. Purchase to satisfy your collection desires, but be careful to buy an authentic piece that is of the age you want.

TAKING CARE OF AND DISPLAYING BEADWORK AND QUILLWORK

Since beadwork and quillwork are usually sewn onto brain-tanned hide or trade cloth, it is vital that they do not get wet. When wet, hide gets hard and discolored, while cloth will bleed and/or shrink; once in that condition, the value is reduced. There are no real ways to restore hide to its original softness once hardened, but some magic solutions can help preserve and slightly soften hard leather. The best protection is not to let moisture on these pieces in the first place. An ounce of prevention is worth a pound of cure!

Quills are very susceptible to insect infestation and should be examined periodically for damage and the piece stored in moth balls for a period of time yearly. One would expect beads to be easily damaged, but actually they are fairly sturdy. After all, consider how much the American Indians used their beaded clothing, and you can see that they are very durable. However, antique pieces are now very old and need to be well cared for.

Displaying your artifacts is the fun part of owning them. Large glass display cases are nice to use but not necessary. The pieces can be hung on walls or laid flat in the open, provided that small hands, pets, and pests are not allowed access to them. Proper hanging is important so that too much stress is not put on any vital area. Long periods of weight on a weak area, or even on a good area, causes that point to stretch and weaken. Careful pinning up (without piercing) of the pieces is important so that the weight is evenly dispersed at all hanging points.

Never display beadwork or quillwork in sunlight, as long periods of exposure cause fading and drying of the hide or trade cloth. While you may not do damage to the beads, you will damage the backings and threads that hold the pieces together.

Also, displaying your collectibles in tight glass frames that are left in the sun will cause condensation inside the frame. Beautiful pipe bags have been ruined due to moisture condensation inside airtight display cabinets.

Beadwork can be professionally cleaned. You can achieve light cleaning with a damp towel or toothbrush, thereby cleaning the beads without getting the backing wet. This method will brighten the beadwork by removing dirt and grime. A soft dry brush applied lightly is good for dusting the pieces. Quillwork can be cleaned the same way, but be sure to use very little moisture. A stiff brush can be used to clean the hide on pieces that have large open areas.

Repair work is more common to beadwork and quillwork than most of us may realize. Ask yourself: If American Indians used the pieces, why aren't any quill or beads missing on most of the gallery and museum quality pieces? The answer is that most fine beadwork is repaired to replace missing beads; the same is true for quillwork. Some pieces are even rebuilt—taking parts from more than one original piece and making one good piece. Careful observation of the connecting stitches will usually show you that rebuilding has taken place. Again, to be safe, buy from a reputable seller, thereby ensuring the authenticity of the piece. Repairs and rebuilding are not financially rewarding on less-expensive pieces, so you will find little or no work done on the more common pieces. However, if you have a piece of beadwork that is damaged, there are professionals available to repair it. It's recommended that you save these old pieces from further deterioration, keeping them for the future.

To temporarily prevent beads from falling off the threads used to stitch them onto a backing, put a tiny drop of glue on the tip of the thread so that the next bead cannot slide off. Be careful not to get glue on the rest of the artifact.

Record keeping on any antique beadwork and quillwork is very important. Any piece with a recognized provenance is very valuable since the majority of collection pieces have no name of maker or user. Good records kept on file cards or in a book with identifying numbers attached to the piece will suffice.

On the written record include the following:

1. type of beaded or quilled piece
2. tribe
3. date of construction
4. name and maker or user, if known
5. name of previous owners
6. price paid
7. appraisal value, if known
8. whether the piece is insured, and with whom
9. photograph(s) of the items

As I have mentioned before, a videotape is an excellent way to keep track of what you own, especially if needed for insurance purposes.

THE MARKET FOR BEADWORK, QUILLWORK, AND OTHER DECORATED PIECES

Due to the limited availability of antique pieces, the market is very firm and advancing. The market on top-quality, rare pieces is very strong, while the intermediate collector pieces are strong. The poorer-quality and easy-to-locate pieces are generally firm but not advancing much in price.

Prices of antique beadwork and quillwork may seem high to the uninformed, but the prices are better understood when compared to other forms of art. Continued supply is no longer being produced and demand is increasing.

What values are put on American Indian beaded and quilled pieces? It may surprise you to know that prices range from the extremes of $100,000 for a spectacular old war shirt to $50 for a contemporary beaded belt buckle. Most pieces trade in the $300 to $3,000 range for antique pieces of quality; poorer-quality pieces run $50 to $300.

REPRODUCTIONS

Unfortunately, there are and have been people making reproductions of old American Indian beadwork and quillwork. Some of the reproductions are poorly done and can be easily distinguished from authentic pieces, but other reproductions are near-perfect and only an expert can tell (and may have trouble telling all the time).

The use of old beads applied to aged, brain-tanned hide, done in traditional style, produces a reproduction that is almost better than the original. This is where collectors must learn all the details of detecting the slightest variations between authentic old pieces and well-made reproductions. Even with all the knowledge you can gather, it is always good to confer with the most knowledgeable person you know before making a large purchase.

Here is how to examine for reproductions. Give the piece an overall general look and determine the following:

1. Does it appear old, showing good patina and proper wear for its designated age?
2. Is the piece constructed from the right materials for the tribe and the supposed age of the piece?
3. Is the piece technically constructed correctly?
4. Does the piece compare to authentic ones correctly?
5. Does any provenance given check out correctly?

Two tools that can help you detect repairs and pieced together artifacts are an ultraviolet light and a 5- or 10-power magnifying glass. An ultraviolet will show repairs and restoration because the new repairs will reflect light differently than will the original areas. Magnification is necessary to examine the sewing, materials, wear, and colors.

One clue found in the marketplace is that a person who makes reproductions will generally make more than one copy. Thus if you suddenly start to see a number of scarce pieces available on the market, take heed. For example, there was a deluge of fine-looking Cheyenne beaded pipe bags recently on the market, all priced about $3,000 and all similar in style.

Usually the makers will not use the traditional materials with reproductions of lesser value. For example, synthetic sinew is often substituted for real sinew. This is an immediate clue that something is wrong when found in supposedly older pieces.

Nothing replaces knowledge of the pieces you are collecting, coupled with buying with guarantees from an honest and reliable seller.

TRIBAL IDENTIFICATION OF BEADWORK

Determining which tribe made an old piece of beadwork can be complicated and frustrating. In many cases there are not enough easily determined differences to pinpoint tribes who did similar work. However, you can usually determine tribal groups such as Central Plains, Southwest, etc. From there, do your best to find the differences between tribes in that group.

I have outlined below a simple system to get beadwork collectors started on learning identification. This system will not make you an expert or even allow you to always identify a piece; it will show you a systematic method to use. Only with further research and years of study will you become good at identification of beadwork.

First, determine the type of bead application that was used. This will help you identify the tribal groups where the piece was made. Second, examine the design and color of beads used to determine a specific tribe. Most tribes used certain designs and colors of beads. Also, look for unique features that are tribal specific. Compare your piece with the details below:

1. Type of bead application
   a. Lazy stitch
      1) The Sioux used rigid bead lanes, while the
         Cheyenne bead lanes lie flat on the surface.
   b. Overlay stitch

      1) Northern Plains tribes
         a) Blackfoot, Assiniboine, Gros Ventre, Sioux, Plains Cree, Sarsi
      2) Plateau tribes
         a) Yakima, Nez Perce, Umatilla, and Flathead
      3) Great Lakes - Prairie area tribes
         a) Chippewa, Santee Sioux, Winnebago, Menominee, Ottawa, Potawatomi, Iroquois, and Huron
      4) Athabascan tribes of Canada and Alaska
         a) All tribes of the area
      5) Northeast tribes
         a) Micmac, Iroquois, Seneca, Delaware, Oneida, Mohawk, Ottawa, and Maliseet

c. Crow stitch
      1) Crow

d. Netted stitch
      1) Southern Plains tribes
         a) Kiowa, Comanche
      2) Southwest tribes
         a) Mojave, Yuma
      3) Northwest tribes
         a) Yakima, Nez Perce
      4) Great Lakes tribes
         a) Chippewa

e. Loom woven beadwork
      1) Great Lakes - Prairie tribes
      2) Southwest - Western tribes
         a) Apache
         b) Some California tribes, such as Pitt River and Washoe

f. Combination of stitches: lazy stitch and overlay
      1) Southern Plains tribes
         a) Southern Cheyenne, Southern Arapaho, Kiowa, Pawnee, and Comanche

2. Determine designs, color of beads, and particulars of style or type

a. Central Plains tribes

1) Sioux: geometric designs, strong central figures
in designs, forms outlined, spidery appendages
after 1870

a) preferred white backgrounds with red,
yellow, and green beads in design

2) Arapaho: geometric designs, stepped triangles,
rectangles, and hexagons with one or two
colored windows

3) Cheyenne: geometric designs, no central figure
in designs, usually preferred smaller size beads,
and liked striped style design. In triangles, the
enclosed rectangle comes all the way to the edge
of the triangle.

4) The Crow designs are very distinct.

a) designs of tall triangles and K-shapes fill the
whole field to decorate

(1) color preference is very expanded to
rose, lavender, light blue, greens, along
with reds, blues, white, and yellows

(2) outline designs with white or blue, sewn in
opposite direction from the background

(3) used blue and red trade cloth as backing,
especially on leggings

b) floral designs after 1900

b. Northern Plains tribes

1) Blackfoot: geometric and floral designs

a) checkerboard design motif, made of small
squares, triangles, or diagonal rows.

b) floral, double curved system, concentric rows
of beads to fill space

c) preferred background of light blue, yellow,
and pink, with multicolors for design

2) Other Northern tribes: similar style with
individual tribal variations

c. Plateau tribes

1) geometric and floral designs

        2) stitch designs: fully beaded backgrounds

        3) prolific makers of flat rectangular bags with flowers, animals, and scenes

        4) used diagonal designs on borders of geometric designs

        5) used all colors

  d. Great Lakes and Prairie tribes

        1) Geometrically, prior to 1800 with floral design popular after 1800

            a) wild rose design very popular, with vines and leaves

            b) some animal shapes including mythical creatures

        2) Woven beadwork is primarily geometric.

        3) Wampum belts were unique to this area.

        4) Outlining with white was done by the Potawatomi.

        5) There were so many tribes and designs that this group requires detailed study that cannot be given here.

  e. Athabascan tribes

        1) Floral after 1850, with geometric prior to 1850. Some tribes did a curvilinear-like geometric design. Designs are usually on moose or reindeer hide. However, they preferred cloth or velvet.

        2) They did not use a background of beads. Colors are bright and consist of almost all colors.

        3) They made types of items that no other tribes made, such as dog blankets, fire bags, game bags, etc.

  f. Eastern tribes

        1) Floral on trade cloth or sometimes hide with nonbeaded background

        2) Scroll and European floral motif

            a) used the double curve design

            b) dainty and fine workmanship

        3) Liked all the colors of autumn; did lines of beads

and edges often in clear beads or white

    4)   Distinctions in designs between tribes such as Micmac and Penobscot are usually in how they did the double-curve motif.

  g. Southern Plains, Southwest, and Western tribes

    1)   Geometric designs

    2)   Southern Plains pieces stand out because:

       a) They used very little beadwork, except to do edging and long narrow lines of beadwork. They preferred to decorate with long hide fringes, metal cones, and painted hide.

       b) They often dyed hide with yellow and/or green ocher.

       c) No quillwork was done.

    3)   The Kiowa tribe did abstract florals with different motifs on the same piece.

    4)   Ute beadwork is distinguished by:

       a) use of trade cloth with full field of beadwork

       b) solidly painted large areas

    5)   The Apache used black beads with yellow and white beads in geometric forms on hide, and did not bead the background area.

    6)   The California tribes did very little beadwork, but the Pitt River tribe did good loom work with geometric designs. The Washoe and Paiute of California and Nevada beaded baskets.

QUILLWORK IDENTIFICATION

The tribal origin of quillwork is very hard to determine. Early quillwork consisted of simple squares, lines, circles, and triangles, thereby leaving very little differences between tribes. Here are a few clues to help you begin learning about quillwork tribes.

Northern Plains tribes such as the Blackfoot, Sarsi, and Crow used very simple bands of wrapping.

Central Plains tribes did geometric quillwork and in the later 1800s did some beautiful animal and human motifs. Delicate floral quillwork on hide, leaving the hide as the background is characteristic of the Santee Sioux of Minnesota. They used quills dyed in light blue, red, yellow, and green. Very early pieces of quillwork were in geometric form but these pieces are rare to find for collection.

In Canada and Alaska the Athabascan tribes were prolific quill workers and produced very fine work. The Cree belts and straps are some of the finest delicate work done in the geometric motifs.

The Micmac, Eastern Chippewa, and other Eastern tribes produced unique birch bark items. The Micmacs quilled boxes, toy cradles, chair covers, table tops, tea cozies, pin cushions, etc. These items are very desirable collectibles and are available, as thousands were made for the tourist trade.

Very rare and expensive is the quillwork done on black buckskin. This is very old and comes from the Great Lakes and Eastern regions; a great find if one gets lucky.

OTHER TYPES OF AMERICAN INDIAN DECORATION

Ribbon work is beautifully executed by many of the American Indian tribes. It is the application of silk cut-out designs onto garments. It was done by tribes from the Great Lakes, Prairie, and Eastern areas. The Potawatomi were the most skillful at ribbon work. Other tribes that did ribbon work were the Kickapoo, Miami, Shawnee, Sauk and Fox, Menominee, Winnebago, Chippewa, Ottawa, Oto, and the Forest Potawatomi.

Moosehair embroidery was not widely done, but when it was the result was magnificent. Pieces periodically show up and are worthy of any collection. Moosehair embroidery was started by the sisters in a Quebec convent and by American Indian girls in the early 1700s. These pieces were made to sell to European tourists. The Huron and Iroquois did most of this work. The hair is 4 to 5 inches long with white and black tips and is collected from a killed moose's rump, mane, and cheeks. The hair is washed and dried like quill, i.e., softened with saliva or water, flattened between the women's teeth, and applied to a backing by bundling three hairs and sewing it onto the backing. Designs lines are straight and zigzag.

Items you find decorated with moose hair are leggings, moccasins, belts, garters, boxes, pouches, knife sheaths, coats, and many tourist items.

Floss embroidery was also practiced by some North American Indian tribes. The use of floss (a hard, twisted silk thread with a sheen) and yarn is seen on moccasins, gauntlets, bags, and many other items. Colors are usually pink, lavender, purple, and green. Before 1850 some floss embroidery was done on hide; after 1850 most was done on cloth.

Northwest Coast toy canoe

5

WOOD AND HIDE COLLECTIBLES

American Indian wood and hide collectibles are mainly from the historic and later periods, as deterioration of older pieces has been prevalent. A few prehistoric items survived in dry caves, permafrost, and mud deposits, but millions of relics that our early American Indians made from wood or hide have perished.

Fortunately, historic artists have been prolific in making wood and hide collectibles that we can still enjoy and collect today.

Wood is a natural product that man has utilized from his very early beginnings. It has been used as a fuel to keep warm, a medium to carve into tools, weapons, and utility items, and for expressions of art. From wood, early man created the atlatl weapon, the club, rabbit sticks, and digging sticks, to name a few. Later man made canoes, masks, bows and arrows, spoons, bowls, cradles, dolls, bull roarers, boxes, statues, wands, quirts, totem poles, and many more items.

American Indian wood collectibles are unique in that from this soft, cellulose material the native people used their ability to originate fine carvings. This allowed their tradition and spirit to enter into the object carved.

Hide from buffalo, deer, elk, antelope, reindeer, moose, bear, caribou, and small animals was a primary source of strong yet flexible material to make clothing, containers, boats, and many other items. The hide artifacts discussed here are nonbeaded and unquilled types such as parfleches, plain hide bags, quivers, and footwear.

PREHISTORIC WOOD ARTIFACTS

Although not many of the wooden objects made by American Indians before contact with the Europeans have survived for us to study, enjoy, and collect, there are still some available.

Old bows and arrows found in dry caves of the Southwest sometimes survived intact. These are usually plain and occasionally painted. Painted ceremonial bows, some of them only 12-18 inches long, have been found and collected. Also discovered in the Southwest are wooden axe handles, rabbit sticks, combs, hair ornaments, awls, digging sticks, smoking tubes, clubs, split-twig fetishes, toys, weaving tools, and whistles. Unique but hard to collect are split-twig fetishes that are hunting fetishes used by the early hunter about 4000 years ago.

In many Southwest collections you will find smoking tubes, also called prehistoric cigarettes. They are made from a small piece of reed cane, and some are decorated with corn husk or twine-like materials. They are very plentiful and inexpensive.

Rabbit sticks are another wooden artifact that are easy to collect at reasonable prices. The rabbit stick is looked down upon as a club to kill the poor creatures, but we may be mistaken; it may originally have been a club used to fend off atlatl darts or foes.

In the Far North and Northwest the prehistoric wooden artifacts come from areas where permafrost or mud slides have preserved the pieces. No doubt an area like the Northwest Coast with millions of trees would be a good wood source for the American Indians. During 1966 through 1981 it was clearly illustrated that in the northern part of Washington the American Indians were great carvers and users of woodmaking tools, containers, and many other wood objects: an archeological team excavated over 40,000 items consisting of many well-preserved wood pieces. Thanks to the layers of midden, clay, and mud, the artifacts were preserved from the now famous Ozette Village site.

In the Far North the permafrost has preserved wooden dolls, bowls, masks, human and animal sculptures, tools, and utensils. Due to the shortage of trees, large wood pieces were rare north of the Yukon.

In the Midwest, Northeast, and Plains areas, it is certain that the prehistoric American Indian used wood extensively to make things, but due to years of deterioration they are gone. Handles for many stone axe heads, celts, and flint knives have perished. Atlatls, clubs, spear shafts, rattles, flutes, masks, and drums are very difficult to collect.

In the South and Southeast some very rare American Indian wood artifacts have been found, but due to their scarcity they are not a common collectible. Masks, wood plaques, human effigies, and animal figures were found in Alabama, Florida, and Oklahoma. The great find in Key Marco, Florida, of hundreds of American Indian wood artifacts in a mire of peat illustrates again that wood was a primary material in the life of early man. Besides furniture, tools, jewelry pieces, masks, and fishing gear made of wood, the fabulous deer ceremonial mask was found with the original paint intact. But again, no wood artifacts from this area are commonly available.

In the West some prehistoric wood artifacts have survived. Examples are clubs, paddles, digging sticks, rabbit sticks, and wood mortars from California, Oregon, and the Great Basin areas.

Historic wood collectibles

Now here is where the collector can really find specimens to acquire. True, some early historical pieces are too rare and expensive, but still there are fewer rare and inexpensive wood collectibles such as kachina dolls, masks, bows, arrow shafts, and many other pieces.

Listed below are wood collectibles by region of origin.

SOUTHWEST

Bows and arrows. Here you will find old Pueblo bows and arrows, as well as Apache, Navajo, Hopi, Zuni, Papago, and Pima. The pieces are distinguishable from each other. For example, most Apache arrows are made with a point that slides out of the shaft.

Bull roarers. This artifact is a flat stick about 5 inches long and 1-1/2 inches wide. A string is attached to one end, and the bull roarer is swung around one's head making a roaring, moaning noise. Navajo-made pieces are available.

Clubs. Plain wood clubs are occasionally available to collect. For some reason not very many have been found in the Southwest.

Cradleboards. Wood cradleboards of the Navajo are collectible. They consist of two backboards laced together and a top board. The Acomas, Second Mesa Hopi, and Zuni also made cradleboards. Wicker cradles were also made by the Hopi and other Pueblo tribes.

Drums and drum sticks. Combined with a hide skin drum face, many older drums are available at affordable prices. Drum sticks are a good collectible even without the drum.

Flutes. Historic flutes are a nice addition to a collection. The Apache made a cane flute with finger holes that is very collectible.

Kachina dance sticks. These are usually in pairs and have birds or other figures on top. They are used in the Hopi kachina dances. Availability is fair.

Kachina dolls. These are wooden dolls made by the Hopi. In the Hopi belief system, the old kachinas are a medium which embody the spirit of things in the Hopi environment and the spirit of those departed. The Hopi believe everything has a spirit. Ceremonially, during the year kachina dances are preformed where the men of the villages impersonate kachinas, wearing masks of the special kachina involved in those dances. There are many different types of kachina dolls that are made from the root of cottonwood trees, painted, and decorated with various items such as hide, bells, yarn, and many other items. The early kachinas were made for Hopi ceremonies and given to the children of the village; they were crude and simple. The entire body of the older kachinas was painted with mineral or vegetal paint, and one can tell in which dance the doll was used by its detail and color. The body is abstract and stands on its own.

Rabbit sticks. These are flat wood sticks about 2-1/2 feet long and 3 to 4 inches wide. They are sometimes lightly carved and are thought to have been used for killing rabbits during the rabbit drives for food.

Rasping sticks. These are sticks with rows of notches cut transversely into the wood. By rubbing another stick or object rapidly back and forth over the notched area, a rattling sound is made. Some rasping sticks are decorated with carved birds and animals on the handled end.

Violins. The Apache violin is made from the stalk of the agave plant. The tubular stalk is hollowed out and closed off at both ends. Holes are made for the noise to resonate out of. One and two strings are stretched from a stick running horizontally through the stalk at the top. At the bottom the strings connect to a small peg. Decorations are applied by painting, etching, and burning on the surface. Violins are available to collect.

Weaver's tools. Today there are a number of people who collect the wood tools used by rug weavers. These include carding paddles, spindles, battens, and combs.

FAR NORTH AND NORTHWEST

The people making wood tools in this area include the Eskimo (Inuits), Athabascans, Tlingit, Haida, Nootka, Kwakiutl, Bella Coola, Salish, and Tsimshian.

Bows and arrows. The Northern tribes made identifiable bows and arrows. For detailed identification of tribe types, refer to *North American Bows, Arrows, and Quivers* (Mason, 1972). The arrows of the Northwest group are tipped with fancy metal, shell, blunt wood, stone, ivory, horn, and plain metal points. Bows are identifiable as to tribe by studying the length, whether sinewed or not, type of wood, designs if any, and shape. Northwestern bows are commonly carved and painted. Eskimo compound bows made of sinew and horn are very sophisticated. Bow strings are made of cotton, twisted sinew, and rawhide strips. Many of the premium quality pieces have been collected and come on the market only periodically, with values increasing.

Boxes. The Northwest American Indians prided themselves on making various types of wood boxes. The purpose for the box dictated its size and shape. They were used for storage, furniture, drums, buckets, cradles, tools, for storing ceremonial paraphernalia, and for sale to the tourist. Boxes of the Northern tribe are more square and squat, while those of the Southern tribe are long and narrow with higher sides. Bentwood boxes are made by steaming and bending the wood and by elaborately carving the sides of these boxes in totemic figures and then painting. The original paint on older boxes is usually worn, but the beautiful patina remains. The Eskimos made numerous small boxes of various types; they are usually round-cornered and decorated with ivory latches and effigy figures which are attached.

Canoe models. These miniature sized canoes are exact copies of the full-sized ones. The wood-frame types are covered with hide, and these canoes are called kayaks and umiaks. A kayak has from one to three manholes for the boatman to sit in, with hide covering the rest of the top. A umiak is open-topped. These models are usually 12 to 36 inches long and are Eskimo made. In the Northwest there is a Northern wood style, opened-topped, and a Southern wood style, open-topped but with a clipper-type bow. The older canoes are available but expensive. If the models have human figures in them, then they become more valuable.

Clappers. These are pieces of wood cut square or round, hollowed out, and wrapped together with fiber. They are hinged and produce a loud noise when shaken. The Kwakiutl tribes made a nicely carved clapper.

Clubs. Various types of clubs from fish killers to war clubs were made. Northwest tribes elaborately carved clubs are beautiful with availability being scarce.

Combs. Wooden combs with carved figures of humans and animals were made by the Northwest tribes. The Eskimos made most of theirs out of ivory, but occasionally made wooden combs. Most Northwest combs are very rare and priced accordingly.

Dance wands. This is a staff used to keep dancers who are wearing masks from getting out of line or falling into the fires near the dance. They are usually carved and/or painted. There are a few available for sale.

Dishes. The Northwest tribes carved wooden dishes. Some were plain and some were elaborately carved with totemic figures. The Eskimos made small food dishes from wood as well as large platterlike dishes.

Drums and drum sticks. Wood-rimmed flat and wood-base box drums were made. Usually totem symbols were painted on the Northwest drums. Eskimo and Athabascans also made drums. Fancy and plain drum sticks are a nice addition to any collection of drums.

Feast bowls. Beautiful wooden food bowls were an important part of Northwest American Indian ceremonial life. Animal effigies were carved into the full shape of the bowl, however plain simple bowls were also carved. Well-crafted bowls are collectible but are getting expensive.

Figurines. Most of the Northwest tribes made figurines. These are elaborately carved, small to large painted effigies of humans and animals. They are rare, and the prices are quite high on these items.

Frontlets. These are forehead masks made by the Northwest tribes. Usually heavily carved with clan crests, they were originally made to wear at ceremonies by high-ranking persons. Availability on the historic pieces is rare.

Halibut hooks. These large circle, bentwood hooks are very desirable to collect and are available. Some are effigy-carved and made from two pieces of wood lashed together.

Helmets and hats. Elaborately carved helmets were originally made as protection in fighting, thus they are sometimes called war helmets. Usually, carved animals were placed on the top of the hat as decoration. Also, ceremonial wooden hats were carved with animal crests and other clan figures placed on top. Both helmets and hats are very rare and hard to collect.

Masks. Of all the Northwest, Eskimo, and Athabascan wood-carved artifacts, masks are the most sought after by the collector. The tradition of mask carving and the use of these masks is as old as the idols and spirits that they depict. Early masks were made for three purposes, (1) for chiefs and high-ranking officials, (2) for ceremonies, and (3) for the shaman and his work. Eskimo masks are different from Northwest masks in form and style. Some are simple wood-carved human faces and dream masks; others are spirit masks with a wooden center and wild appendages attached. It was only after 1850 that masks of the Northwest were being made for sale to the public. Pre–1900 masks are very scarce and few are available to collect, unless another collector is willing to sell one, and then the price will be in the thousands of dollars. Masks made in the 1920s are available to collect.

Mat creasers. These are handled, crescent-shaped wooden tools used in sewing bark mats. They have a groove at the lower edge which, when held over the sewing needle as it is withdrawn prevents the needle hole from being too large. They are sometimes highly carved and other times plain. Some of these mat creasers do come onto the market occasionally.

Oil dishes. These were smaller dishes carved with animal figures. Dried fish and other foods were dipped into the grease held by these dishes. Some are inlaid with shell and/or teeth.

Paddles. Beautifully carved and/or painted, full size and miniature, canoe paddles are popular as collectibles. Both Northwest and Eskimo tribes made paddles. Availability is good.

Pipes. Elaborately carved Northwestern wood pipes are something special. They are usually totemic figures carved in high-relief with a copper- or metal-lined bowl. The Eskimo also made great pipes with large curved wooden stems that have a small metal or stone bowl on top. There are also lead- to wood-fitted Eskimo pipes. Collectors will find the Eskimo pipes less expensive and more available than the fancy carved Northwest pipes.

Rattles. The Northwest tribes made wood-carved rattles that are very desirable. Totemic figures cover these rattles. The Raven Rattles with humans riding on top are masterpieces of work. Prices for the Raven Rattles have risen sharply. Availability of less fancy wood-carved rattles is only fair.

Speaker sticks. This is the badge of office for the spokesman of the chief. Speaker sticks resemble small slender totem poles.

Spoons. There are wooden ceremonial and common day utilitarian spoons carved by the Northwest tribes. Elaborately carved with totemic figures, they served as food servers at feasts. Larger feast ladles with animal heads were also used. Prices will be high for the older pieces. Feast spoons were usually carved in pairs with the same decorations, however it is hard to find these matching pairs. Eskimo wooden spoons are less decorative.

Totem poles. These are huge cylindrical carved poles displaying family and tribal crests or coats of arms, made by the Northwest coast tribes. They are read from top to bottom, and on old poles one could read them to ascertain the intermarriages of families. Totem poles were put in front of graveyards, meeting places, and homes. Animal forms carved in relief, such as birds, fish, humans, and demon-like masks were stacked on top of each other. Medium size and miniature totem poles were also made, and the tourist-type small poles have become quite collectible.

Whistles. Wood-carved whistles were used by the Northwest tribes and occasionally one will pop up for collection. They were originally made to be blown to announce the coming of the ceremonial seasons. There are different types producing different sounds. One, two, and three shaft types were made, each with several holes and reeds for the sounds. Some whistles show fancy carvings of totemic figures and others have painted designs.

PLAINS, GREAT LAKES AND EASTERN AREAS

These three large areas consolidate nicely because they used similar wood artifacts yet shaped and decorated them differently.

Backrests. The Plateau and Plains American Indians made a piece of collectible furniture, the backrest. Looking like a long triangular hammock, a backrest is made of many horizontal, straight willow sticks lashed together down the middle and the two sides with three strings of sinew or cordage. The edges and the top are covered with cloth or hide. Decoration may be beadwork, shells, or metal dangles. It can be used for a backrest or bed. Backrests are available to collect, but the older ones can be hard to find.

Bows and arrows. Bows were made of hardwood such as yew, ash, hickory, and Osage orange and were mainly single pieces of wood. An exception is the compound bow of the Sioux. This bow was made of three pieces of buffalo or sheep horn covered with hide or cloth. Arrows are made and marked in such a manner that the experienced person can distinguish both the tribe and the artist. Most Plains arrows have grooves going down the sides and are fletched at two or three locations. The points attached by sinew are metal, stone, or wood. The shafts are made of hardwood. Bows and arrows are very sought after and prices have been rising.

Birch bark items. The Great Lakes and Eastern area American Indians lived with and expertly used the birch tree. From these trees came the bark of which many collectibles are made including canoes, buckets, cradles, baskets, moose calls, boxes, tobacco trays, comb cases, floats, and various tourist items. Birch bark collectibles are plentiful and very reasonably priced.

Canes. Some tribes prided themselves on making canes similar to walking canes with handles often being carved with a face or other figures.

Clubs. The American Indians of the Plains, Great Lakes, and Eastern areas made the following types of clubs mostly used in war.

> **Simple.** The earliest plain wooden clubs were of straight shafts, wider at the distant end with a grip area at the top. One example of a simple club is a branch with a burl at one end.

> **Hardwood ball head.** In the Great Lakes and Eastern areas hardwood clubs with a round ball on the club end and with a narrow handle were made. These can be plain, heavily carved,

and sometimes effigy-carved. One or more metal points were often inset into the wooden head to make the club more lethal. The Penobscot made a club from the roots of the birch tree which is usually carved with effigy figures.

Gunstock. The shape of this club is like a gunstock. These wooden clubs are flat and about 3/4 to 1 inch thick. At the end of the club, 1-3 metal spikes or horn are usually inserted, although some gunstock clubs are made of wood only. The club can be painted or carved. Quite often strings of beads, quills, or feathers are attached to the handle. These were mainly from the Great Lakes, Eastern and Northern Plains areas.

Fixed stone head. These are war clubs with a ball- or egg-shaped stone head. A wood shaft with wrapped rawhide is attached to it. The length can be from 2 to 4 feet. They are very lethal and extremely effective from horseback. Most Plains tribes used this type of club.

Slingshot. This club has a small stone head covered by rawhide with about 2 inches of flexible hide between the head and a wooden handle covered with hide. This hingelike attachment allows the head to sling back and forth when in use. The Ute, Apache, Oto, Nez Perce, Sioux, and Blackfoot liked this type of club.

Decorated and ceremonial. These are fixed stone-headed clubs with beadwork around the stone head and down the shaft. The head is oversized and the handle short. Instead of beads to decorate, sometimes braided horsehair is used. The handle is occasionally painted. A ceremonial staff-type club is also classified under this category; these were made strictly for dances and other ceremonies. They may have a pair of horns or a stone head decorated with beads, horsehair, or paint. They are also called wands.

Effigy head. Sculpturally carved, soft stone heads were produced depicting humans and animals, as were wood-carved club heads with human faces, a very choice collectible. Further decoration on the wooden heads was done with cobbler tacks and larger brass tacks. Any of the above clubs were also commonly decorated with strings of beads, feathers, or trade items. In fact, tacking and carving of the large wooden clubs was very popular. Collectibility of effigy-head clubs is poor due to the scarcity.

Clubs are very collectible. Some of the fancy ball and gunstock clubs are expensive but so exciting to own. Fixed-head clubs are very available, but the prices have been inching up during the last few years.

Cradleboards. Wooden cradles were used by the Great Lakes and Eastern tribes such as the Iroquois and the Seneca. These cradles are large flat boards with a footboard at the bottom, small wooden sides, and a hoop board. Usually fancy carving and paint is used to decorate these old boards.

Crooked knife handles. The crooked knife was made for carving wood. The carvers took time to make beautiful handles to hold the metal blades. Simple crooked wood handles to animal and human head handles were made. These are very collectible.

Cutting boards. Tobacco was cut on boards that were often nicely carved. Availability is fair for collecting.

Drums and drum sticks. Both one-faced and two-faced, from small hand drums to large dance drums, American Indians liked the sound resonating from them. There are also a few two-faced, square, plain drums made. Designs are often painted on the hide top and on the wood which makes up the sides. Very collectible too are the drum sticks used to produce the sound. Some sticks are decorated by beading the heads, some are quilled or carved, and some are plain.

Flutes. To court a woman, it was the practice for the young American Indian man to play love songs on his flute. A flute is made of wood, usually red cedar, elder, and other woods with large pithy centers. The branch is cut in half and the pith removed, except for one end. The two halves are put back together wrapped with hide strips or animal intestines, and holes are made on top for the fingers. At the mouth end a hollow rectangular piece of wood is tied over the top hole called a stop. This wood stop has a curved piece of tin placed under it, and sometimes these stops are carved with an animal or bird head. At the far end from the mouth, a bird's beak is often depicted. Flutes were common with nearly all the tribes of this area. Finding and collecting an old flute is possible if one is willing to pay a good price.

Feast bowls. The Great Lakes and Eastern tribes are known for their wooden feast bowls. The fancy carved effigy bowls are of better quality and have finer art work than those made elsewhere. Beautiful animal heads such as horses are often seen on the rims of these dark patina-covered bowls. Eastern Sioux, Chippewa, Winnebago, Sauk and Fox, Potawatomi, and other tribes were a few who made these fantastic bowls. Generally, the Plains and Northern Plateau tribes made simpler bowls, however some effigy bowls were made. Availability is limited, but they can be secured for a price.

Heddles. This is a wood, ivory, or bone form made to hold the threads for weaving narrow pieces such as sashes by the small holes drilled down the middle slats. The edges were often carved. Collectors seldom see heddles for sale.

Lacrosse sticks. The Iroquois played the game of lacrosse. Wooden sticks with long handles and a netlike structure at one end were used. Not many are on the market but prices are good.

Ladles. Wooden ladles were made by the Eastern and Great Lakes tribes and a few by the Plains tribes. Effigy figures were often carved.

Masks. The Iroquois made the well-known False Face and Husk Face masks. The False Faces came about as masks to wear to satisfy supernatural beings encountered in the forest. The masks have mouths with variable features, eyes that are deep-set and often surrounded with tin or brass, and noses that are large and sometimes bent. The eyebrows are wrinkled and divided longitudinally by a crease. Horsehair provided hair for the mask as did buffalo mane, braided cornhusk, and shredded basswood. Masks are classified by feature variation. The types are spoon-lipped, smiling, crooked mouth, protruding tongue, divided, long nose, horned and whistling. They also made animal masks and a blind mask with no eyes. The Seneca tribes made similar masks but in limited numbers. For dance ceremonies, the Cherokees made Booger Masks of wood. These masks consist of human and animal faces with hair added to make the mask more realistic. One type of Cherokee

Booger Mask has a human wearing a coiled rattlesnake on his head. Collectibility of the Iroquois and Cherokee masks is good.

Mortars and pestles. Wooden mortars and pestles were used in the Plains, Great Lakes, and Eastern areas. Occasionally a well-preserved piece finds it way to the market.

Quirts. A quirt is a decorated wooden handle with a leather strap attached which is used as a horse whip. Decoration of the handle may be done with tacks, cut-out shapes, or carvings.

Pipe stems. To the American Indian the pipe is one of the most important items in his spiritual and ceremonial world. Pipe stems are also called calumets. They were made of wood, reed, and sometimes bone. Pipes stems after 1880 are available to collect. Pre–1880 pipes stems are hard to locate. Here are a few types of historical pipes stems for collection:

> **Flat.** The wood stem is flat, 1-1/2 to 3 inches wide and usually 22–36 inches long. Decoration of the flat stem consists of carving in relief, cutouts, wrapping of beads and/or quill, brass tacking, horsehair and duck feather additions, hot-file burn markings, paint work, and inlaid lead or catlinite. Many nice flat pipe stems are simple with no design but have great patina from usage.

> **Twisted.** These are long, carved, spiral-twisted stems. They were used by the Eastern tribes since the early 1800s.

> **Puzzle.** The route that the smoke travels in a puzzle stem is the secret of the maker. The indirect route of the smoke channel was made by removing part of the flat stem and channeling the hole with a hot wire. The large removed piece was later glued back on. These are usually made with cut-out designs along with any other type of decoration desired by the maker. Lengths are 25-40 inches and about 2-3 inches wide. The Santee Sioux were great makers of the puzzle stem.

> **Fancy carved.** A few fancy carved stems were made, some with free-floating discs on an open wood column; others were long rectangular-shaped stems with a narrow stem down the middle.

Collectability of pipe stems is good, and prices have advanced considerably.

Pipe tampers. Small, narrow wood pipe tampers are fun to collect and reasonably inexpensive. Occasionally a fancy carved pipe tamper is located for collection.

Rattles. Wood rattles were used by most of the tribes, however hide and wood rattles combined were the most common. One style of Plains American Indian rattles has a buckskin-covered stick and pieces of animal hooves attached that rattle when shaken. The most typical Plains rattles are rawhide-headed with wood handles. Birch bark rattles were made by the Iroquois. Gourd rattles made of gourds, hide, and wood were made by the Kiowa, Wichita, and Comanche.

Spoons. The Plains American Indians made most of their spoons out of horn except for the occasional wooden one. The Great Lakes and Eastern tribes made beautiful wide wooden spoons with short handles that were commonly decorated with carved animals and human figures. Collectibility is good with prices high on the well-carved older pieces.

WESTERN AREAS

The main collectible wood artifacts in the West are:

Bows and arrows. The Yurok and Hupa tribes of Northern California made bows of yew wood, broad yet thin in the middle with the ends of the bow tapered and turned back. On the older bows the backs were lined with glued-on sinew to strengthen the bow. Simple California bows are plain and 34 feet long with tapered ends. Some of the Shoshone used this type of bow also. California bows are very collectible. Prices are inching up as these weapons have been underpriced in the past.

Bowls. Simple wooden bowls were made by the California Indians, however the beautiful effigy carving work was produced along the Columbia River by the Wasco and Winham tribes.

Clubs. Simple, long sticklike clubs are found in some collections of

Western artifacts. Along the Columbia River a few carved clubs have been collected.

Mortars. Tall cone-shaped, flat-bottomed wooden mortars were more common than we realize as most have perished. However, later historical wooden mortars of the Columbia River tribes are collectible. Some made by the Wasco tribe are ornately carved with figures. Collectors can still acquire these mortars at high prices.

Mush paddles. These paddles are for stirring mush, soups, and other liquids. They can be small or large. The main tribes who used mush paddles were the Yurok and the Hupa. Not many paddles come on the market, but they are a nice addition to any collection.

Pipes. Fairly rare but still available are wooden pipes of the Northern California tribes. The Pomo made a long rodlike, stemmed pipe with a bulb-shaped bowl. The Yurok and the Hupa made a tube-shaped pipe with a steatite inset bowl.

Spoons. Most Western spoons are made of horn, however some California Yurok and Hupa spoons are carved from wood. Availability to collectors is scarce.

Stick games. Various stick games were played by the Western tribes. Most games consist of sticks of various lengths.

HIDE COLLECTIBLES

There are a number of artifacts made purely from hide with no beadwork or quillwork. Some of the hide collectibles are shields, moccasins, boots, rattles, horse gear, and knife sheaths, to name a few.

Three types of leather were used by the American Indians—brain-tanned, parfleche, and harness. Brain-tanned leather is typical American Indian leather which turns white and soft, lending itself to beading or quilling; animal brain matter and a liquid is used in a process to tan the hide. Parfleche is partially cured leather, and harness leather is European leather used by the American Indians.

Parfleche is a French word used in the American Indian artifact world to describe four types of partially cured leather-hide containers. What distinguishes parfleche leather from brain-tanned hide is that the parfleche is not tanned but soaked in water and stretched on sticks driven into the ground. Buffalo hides were used until replaced with cowhide. The stretched hide is scraped to remove its hair and flesh and to even up the thickness.

American Indian women painted geometric designs on the wet hide, and after it was painted, containers were cut out. The types of containers made were envelopes, boxes, tubular cases, and side-fringed bags. The designs used attribute it to a specific tribe. The Crow tribe at one time etched geometric figures into the hide. Parfleche artifacts are very collectible.

Shields are very hard to collect due to scarcity and price. There are true old war shields, dance shields, and Wild West-type shields. Shields are made from the thickest part of the buffalo hide which is cut out and steamed causing it to shrink and thicken. A thin hide cover is placed over the thick hide shield to protect it and for display of its designs. Warriors made shield cover designs from their mystical dreams. Actual shields are almost impossible to find anymore.

Plain undecorated moccasins and boots worn by the Southwest tribes are collectible today.

Knife sheaths made of hide only and decorated with brass or silver studs similar to those made by the Blackfoot are beautiful and rare. These are usually made from old harness leather acquired from the white man.

The Apache made plain pouches and saddle bags, decorated by painting geometrical designs and/or cut-out decoration where repeated pieces of leather are removed. The edges of pouches and saddle bags were also decorated with hide fringe.

Plain shirts made of brain-tanned leather were often seen in the Southwest. The Taos, Apache, and Comanche tribes were makers of this type of clothing.

CONSTRUCTION AND TECHNIQUE

In woodworking, the main method of carving was to rough out the figure to be carved with stone adzes and to finish it with stone blades or knives. Final smoothing was done by sanding the surface. Some wooden pieces were left unpainted, others were painted. Treatment of the unpainted pieces was accomplished with natural oils and stains.

In addition to stone adzes, stone blades, and knives, other tools used in woodworking were axes, drawshavers, and chisels; in the Northwest, a sanding medium such as sharkskin was used.

The most common types of wood used were:

Southeastern Alaska and Canada: birch, willow, spruce, cedar, and maple

Southwest: cottonwood, willow, mesquite, and agave stems

Northwest: cedar, yew, and alder

Southern: hickory, ash, walnut, and oak

Plains, Great Lakes, and East: maple, hickory, oak, ash, walnut, willow, and birch

Western: willow, yew, spruce, oak, and redwood

In hide work, the skins—after processing either by brain tanning or simple parfleche curing—are cut into the shapes needed to make clothing, weaponry, bags, and other items necessary to daily life. Sewing the pieces together was done with sinew and later cotton thread or by lacing the leather together with thin strips of hide. Some sewing machines were made available to the American Indians by 1885.

The types of hide used were buffalo, deer, antelope, bear, moose, reindeer, elk, and various small mammals.

COLLECTING WOOD AND HIDE

Although prehistoric wood and hide artifacts have mainly disappeared due to deterioration, there are many historic pieces to collect. Most collectors have a few wood or hide artifacts which they usually mix in with other collectibles. The collector of Northwest American Indian artifacts is usually heavily into wood carvings, because the bulk of the Northwest tribes' collectibles are of wood. There is plenty of room for more collectors in the wood and hide collectibles field.

In hide artifacts there are collectors specializing in parfleche pieces. Prices have increased rapidly in the last few years due to publicity about these collectibles, but there are still plenty to collect. Be sure when buying parfleche containers that you know which ones are old and which are new. Older pieces show some wear, patina, and true traditional designs.

Locating these artifacts to collect is not any harder than any other American Indian collectible or antique. Work with reputable dealers, galleries, stores, auction houses, antique stores, and other collectors. The fun of collecting is the hunt for the artifact as well as the possession.

Trading with other collectors is a good source of upgrading one's collection. It will be difficult to locate early historic American Indian wooden art forms, but they are out there, especially in old collections, galleries, and in dealer's inventories.

Determine the best quality when purchasing. The better-quality art always escalates in price and is easier to sell or trade later. You can determine the best quality by considering the following:

Wood items

1. Be sure the piece is American Indian, true to tradition in design, color, style, and form, and is the proper age and type of wood used.
2. Determine that the craftsmanship is good to excellent. Avoid crude work and/or poor painting.
3. The piece should be pleasing to the eye.
4. Be sure there is no damage or restoration.

Hide items

1. Be sure the piece is the proper age and is true to the American Indian tribe to which it is attributed.
2. Be sure the art work is traditional and of the best craftsmanship.
3. Be sure the condition is good and no restoration has been done.
4. Be sure the leather has little or no damage.

CARING, STORING, AND MARKETS

Caring for wood collectibles mainly involves keeping them away from wood-boring insects and keeping them dry. Direct sunlight will not affect them immediately but will tend to fade the paint and dry out the wood over a long period of time.

More pieces have been damaged by pets chewing on them or small hands playing with them. Good cabinets for display are recommended with locks on the doors. The only cleaning required will be a periodic dusting. In earthquake areas, collectibles such as kachinas will be safer in cabinets with a small amount of Tacky Wax on the bottom of the dolls to hold them in place.

Hide collectibles should be stored out of the hot sun or direct harsh lights. Definitely do not allow moisture on or near hide artifacts. Insects like leather and will attack most pieces. Otherwise, use the same precautions as for wood collectibles.

Market condition for wood collectibles is good. An appraisal is wise and inexpensive. Insurance is expensive but a necessary thing if the proper premium can be secured. Again, pictures or videotape recording of the pieces is recommended.

The market is strong for authentic quality hide pieces.

REPRODUCTIONS

Like most antiques we collect of any value, reproductions of both wood and hide American Indian artifacts are in the marketplace.

Wood and hide are soft materials easier to reproduce than other items such as baskets. Very rare, expensive wood pieces should always be checked by an expert before you conclude a deal. Parfleche containers are commonly reproduced. Some are newer American Indian-made pieces meant for the contemporary market, and others are non-American Indian meant to deceive the buyer. For an old parfleche, be sure it has patina, wear, and a guarantee.

Navajo weaving

6

AMERICAN INDIAN WEAVINGS

HISTORY

Man's early weavings were made out of the necessity for the essentials of life. The need for warmth, storage containers, carrying containers, and bedding caused the first American people to create weavings.

Archaeological evidence of the first man-made weavings in North America are difficult to find, as fabric deteriorates. However, the tools used to weave have been found, aiding in the study of early American Indian weaving.

For example, Prehistoric American Indians of the Midwest had tools for weaving as evidenced by the archaeological finds of the Hopewell and Mississippian Cultures. In the Northwest old spindle whorls of shell and wood were found indicating that weaving had begun fairly early in this region.

In the Southwest there are archaeological finds of weaving tools and a few woven fragments. Due to the dry climate, these are quite plentiful. In dry caves pieces of cotten fabrics with finely woven geometric patterns have been recovered and dated to 300–700 CE. Other objects found were bags and sandals.

American Indian groups who wove were from the Great Lakes, Midwest, Northeast, Northwest, Prairie, Southwest, and West Coast. The availability of wool from the mountain goat and dog may have influenced the Northwest tribes to weave, while the plentifulness of hemp, nettle fibers, and moosehair may have been an influence for the Great Lakes tribes. Certainly, access to the cotton plant and later sheep wool inspired the Southwest tribes to become interested in weaving. Rabbit fur blankets were woven and limited to California, the Northwest, and the Southwest.

With the exception of the Great Lakes tribes who wove highly decorated pieces, early weaving was mostly very plain-looking. As the American Indians began to establish agricultural communities they found they had more time available for weaving and pottery making. As a result their work became finer, and the incorporation of designs more important.

In the Great Lakes area, materials used for weaving during these early times were mostly of vegetable fiber woven on a simple rod where the warps were strung and the wefts woven spirally around them. Sometimes wool of the moose or buffalo was added to the weft to form the design. Many of the early fiber bags had elaborate designs of "thunderbirds" and "underwater panthers"; other weavings had geometric designs as well as animal forms. The elaborate fiber panel bag was eventually replaced with a banded woolen bag, even though the fiber woven bag was still in use until late in the 19th century. Woven bags with figure designs were made until the 1930s.

The Great Lakes tribes as well as some of the Northeast tribes and Prairie tribes made sashes, belts, burden straps, and containers. Woolen blankets traded from the European traders were unraveled and used in the 18th century to weave some bags. Later, Germantown, Saxony, and Bayeta fibers were used for the same purposes. Some of the tribes that practiced weaving are the Chippewa, Potawatomi, Winnebago, Menominee, Sauk and Fox, as well as most of the other Great Lakes and Eastern Prairie tribes. In the East the Huron, Iroquois, and the New England Algonquians did some weaving.

Beautiful handwoven Great Lakes sashes of wool are available to collect today. The fiber panel and banded woolen bags, however, are limited in availability.

The women of the Northwest tribes have woven for centuries. The main natural materials used to weave were mountain goat wool, dog wool, sea otter fur, and cedar bark fibers.

The woven item the Northwest American Indians are best known for is the Chilkat blanket. Made by the Chilkats of the Tlingit tribe, this is a fine example of one style of blanket. Chilkat blankets date from the early 1800s to the early 1900s. Aprons, tunics, and leggings were also woven by the Tlingit.

Robes of yellow cedar bark were used by the Nootka and Kwakiutl groups. These are very early pieces made for personal use and often traded with other tribes of the Northwest. These robes are very rare and not a collectible item today.

The area most associated with American Indian weaving is the Southwest. The ancient Anasazi, Mogollon, Fremont, and Hohokam were fine textile weavers as well as basket makers. Finely woven fabrics of cotton fiber with geometric designs have been found in the Southwest. The Pueblo tribes, following the example of these early people, have become very good weavers, using the upright loom and cotton for yarn.

The Navajo people of the Southwest are not related to the Pueblo people. The Navajo are Athabascans who came down from Alaska and Canada and generations later arrived in the Southwest to settle. However, through their close association with the Pueblo tribes, they learned how to weave.

Spanish weavers of the Rio Grande area (along the Rio Grande River of New Mexico) were making fine weavings at the same time as the Navajo were developing into weavers. From the Rio Grande weavers the Navajo took inspiration and were influenced by their designs, even though the Rio Grande people wove on a parallel loom and the Navajos wove on an upright loom.

The biggest change to affect the Navajo and other weavers of the area was the introduction of sheep by the Spanish. Sheep were ideally adapted to the desert brush lands of the Southwest, converting desert grasses to wool for weaving and providing meat to eat. By the 1700s both the Pueblo and Navajo tribes were using wool in their weavings.

The Navajo in the early 1700s began to weave for trade to other tribes. Most of the early Navajo blankets were simple striped blankets. The earliest recovered Navajo weavings were found at Massacre Cave in Canyon De Chelly in 1805 and were striped blanket fragments made from wool.

By the early 1800s expanding trade routes brought dyes and Bayeta cloth that the weavers could use to add color and fineness to their work. The Bayeta was unravelled, respun, and woven into fine blankets.

The time period from 1850 to 1868 is known as the Classic Weaving Period in the trade. The Navajo moved from making utilitarian clothing in the early part of this period to striped blankets, colorful designed serapes, beautiful "Chief's blankets," and "Child-wearing blankets" in the middle and later part of this period.

Unfortunately, in 1863 Kit Carson and his troops gathered the Navajo and took them to an encampment called Basque Redondo. Many Navajo died on the so-called Long Walk to the Camp in the plains of New Mexico. In 1868, after signing a treaty, the Navajo were allowed to return to their original lands. During these five years of incarceration some weaving was done, but mainly under the instructions of the Spanish. It was after this time, however, that the Navajo produced many weavings, and pieces became more common in both private collections and in museums.

The Pueblo tribes continued to make utilitarian cloth items until they could trade for them at the trading posts. The traditional weavings made by the Pueblo people consisted of blankets, dresses, blouses, mantas, kilts, leggings, sashes, vests, shirts, straps, and stockings.

The Hopi and Zuni tribes of the Pueblo group are the main ones who made some commercial weaving to sell. The other Pueblo tribes made their own ceremonial pieces and items of necessity.

The next period of weaving was the Transitional Period from 1868 to 1890. During this time the Navajo were changing their weaving from blankets to rugs. The pieces woven seemed to be neither blankets nor rugs, so were called transitional. Except for the Hopi, the Pueblo tribes did not make this transition.

The rug period came next from 1890 to 1920, and produced volumes of rugs made for resale. It was during this period that the white traders brought tremendous influence to bear on rug design in order to make them more marketable. Regional area style of rugs in the Southwest were developed during this period.

The major differences between Pueblo and Navajo weavings are:

1. The type of loom and weave used were different. The weave used by the Pueblo people was a 50/50 plain weave and a twill weave; the Navajo used the tapestry weave.
2. Pueblo men did most of the weaving, while women wove for the Navajo.
3. The Navajo changed from weaving blankets to rugs, while the Pueblo, with the exception of the Hopi, did not.

TYPES OF WEAVINGS

There are many types of native weavings. The blanket is one of the earliest and most desirable to collect.

NORTHWEST BLANKETS

In the Northwest the American Indians were weaving blankets on a loom beginning as early as the late 1700s. The first blankets were of limited designs and made from yarn spun from mountain goat wool, sea otter fur, and cedar bark strands. The shapes of the early blankets were squarish with a V-shaped bottom and some were rectangular, wider than long. Most of the blankets had fringe on the sides and bottom.

Geometric designs soon appeared, followed by the design depicting clan crest figures that was unique to the Chilkat blanket.

It is said that the Tsimshian invented the Chilkat blanket. When they were assimilated into the Northern Tlingit tribe about the 1830s, they changed the design from geometric to curvilinear clan crest figures. These designs were provided by the men of the tribe to the women by painting the design on spiral pattern boards for the women to copy. The old geometric blankets were sometimes called *raventails*.

These rare and hard-to-find Chilkat blankets can be identified by their sharp division of art work and the material used. The shape is wider than long with a straight top and a convex bottom with fringe. The framed central design is usually divided into three zones. The middle zone is the most prominent and is best visible when the blanket is worn over the shoulders. The two side zones are symmetrically done with minor motifs and also have a fringe. The materials used to make the blanket are distinguishable also: the warps are of goat wool and cedar bark, while the weft is of white, blue, yellow, and black wool. Some attempts were made in the early 1900s to weave Chilkats with commercial yarn, however, the product was very inferior to the earlier blankets.

Collecting Northwest blankets will be very difficult. Finding blankets earlier than the Chilkat is impossible. And with the value of the antique Chilkat blanket at $30,000-$40,000, and the availability very close to nil, few are collectible.

SOUTHWEST BLANKETS

The Navajo

The greatest blankets ever woven on the North American continent were made between 1830 and 1870 by the Navajo of the Southwest. The early Navajo blankets were striped. Some were shoulder blankets, wider than long, and others were longer than wide.

By the early part of the 1800s, the serape blanket made its appearance. This early Classic Period weaving was a longer than wide blanket, terraced horizontally with designs in red, white, and blue. It was used for wearing and for sleeping.

There are four types of regular sized serape blankets and a child's serape, known as a "child's blanket." You can easily distinguish between each type by design differences and yarn used. By distinguishing the types, you can determine the age.

> 1820–1850: Integrated design. Has an overall pattern of large terraced designs integrated with one another, spreading from the middle of the serape. The Navajo used handspun wool yarn of natural white, indigo blue, and raveled yarn of red bayeta.

1850–1865: Three-zone design. The Navajo used three distinct zones of design. Each zone has wavy bands replacing the integrated design of the earlier period and is separated by a broad area of color that has thin stripes or terraced, wavy band designs. Again, the Navajo used handspun wool yarn of natural white and raveled yarn of indigo blue with the red yarn of either bayeta or sometimes saxony.

1865–1875: Vertical meandering design. Vertical meandering lines replaced horizontal wavy bands. Diagonal, fine terraced lines and figures were included in the design as well as crosses and Xs. Handspun natural white wool yarn is used with indigo blue, saxony red, raveled bayeta, and sometimes green. Later many colorful yarns were used.

1875–later: Transitional serape types. The Navajo took on the overall pattern similar to the earlier serapes but used different figures that were not as integrated into the design. Synthetically dyed red wool yarn with handspun natural white with orange, yellow, green, and indigo blue yarn was used.

Another distinct type of Navajo serape is the Moki serape, the same size and shape as the regular serapes. The difference is that the Moki serape has a background field of blue indigo stripes accomplished by stripes of natural brown, white, and gray. Later about 1860, red bayeta and saxony yarn stripes were included when serrated and terraced design elements were put on the top of the stripes. The Moki serape is very collectible and rare, with prices in the very high range.

Children's serapes are just smaller-size serapes. Pre-1860 child serapes are rare. The Child's blanket is very desirable and a valuable collectible.

Most collectors can associate better with the type of Navajo blankets called Chief's blankets. These blankets are always wider than long and were worn around the body. The name "Chief's" originates from the fact that the Plains Indian chiefs and their families cherished these blankets and traded with the Navajo for them. Chief's blankets are finely woven masterpieces, conservative in use of color and balanced in design. A Chief's blanket is made so that when the four corners are folded to meet in the center, the design is the same as when unfolded. There are five types of these blankets.

For the sake of simplicity and understanding and unless mentioned otherwise, the blue yarn will be homespun indigo blue dyed natural wool; red will be unraveled bayeta or saxony yarn, and white, black, and brown yarn will be homespun natural wool.

1. Ute-style First Phase. This blanket is a direct offspring of the early Navajo shoulder blanket. It is a rectangular, wider than long blanket. It can vary in size but is usually about 60 by 80 inches. It is distinguished by broad stripes of white, blue, and brown or black.

2. First Phase Chief. This blanket is similar to the Ute First Phase except now you have red stripes incorporated into the design, and sometimes the outlining of the broad stripes is done in blue.

3. Second Phase Chief. This blanket is similar to the First Phase Chief's blanket, except that the broader blue stripes will be interrupted by 12 smaller, divided rectangles with 6 placed in the top two stripes and 6 in the bottom two. The Second Phase Chief's blankets are also very rare and expensive to collect but do become available for a price.

4. Third Phase Chief. This is the same as the Second Phase Chief's blanket except the rectangles become a strong central diamond with terraced half and quarter diamonds surrounding it. The central figure is superimposed on the striped pattern. The Third Phase Chief's blanket has great visual effect and is more available to collect.

5. Chief Variant: After 1865, boxes of red Xs, hourglass figures, and crosses appeared superimposed on the striped field of the earlier Chief's blankets. Because these elements are a variant of the older Chief's blankets, they are called Chief Variants.

The women's version of the Chief's blanket is smaller in size with no white stripes. Instead, the narrower stripes are gray and brown.

Some single and double saddle blankets were woven by the Navajo prior to 1865. Most saddle blankets were of twill weave with simple striped designs. A few fancy saddle blankets were made with more elaborate designs and fringe.

After returning from imprisonment at Basque Redondo, the Navajo weavers went through serious changes. Due to the shortage of good wool, the weavers started to use more commercial yarn.

About 1870 Germantown yarn, a commercial product made in Germantown, Pennsylvania, became available to the Navajo. Germantown yarn came in many bright colors. The use of four-ply yarn and synthetic dyes marks the beginning of the Transitional Weaving Period. Now the Navajo had the full spectrum of colors available to them.

A favorite weaving for collectors is the Germantown weaving. You can distinguish it by its very bright colors and tight, fine weave of four- and later three-ply yarn. Its availability to collectors is good, however, prices are fairly high on the better pieces.

Transitional Period weavings are usually very colorful with no borders and are soft to the touch. Early Transitional weavings have design elements similar to Classic pieces, while late Transitional weavings were usually done in synthetic, brightly dyed yarns with later period designs.

After 1880 Navajo pictorial weavings appeared. Included in this group are the Sandpainting, Yeis, Yeii'bicheii, and other pictorial weavings. Prices range from many thousands of dollars to the low hundreds, and availability is good.

Pueblo and Rio Grande blankets

Two other groups wove blankets during the 1700s and 1800s. They were the Pueblo Indians of New Mexico and Arizona and the Spanish settlers of the Rio Grande River area of New Mexico. I mention these two groups because you need to be able to distinguish their blankets from the Navajo.

Pueblo blankets of the early historic period were mainly shoulder blankets. They were woven by men and were more wide than long. Very few of these old Classic Pueblo blankets exist.

The two main weaver tribes in the Pueblo group were the Hopi and the Zuni. The plaid blanket of the Hopi and Zuni were made into the 1900s. Also, fine rugs were woven by the Pueblo people but in less quantity than the Navajo and are now mainly sold to the collector.

Rio Grande weavings also have similarities to Navajo and Pueblo weavings. Beautiful blankets were made in the 1880s that collectors cherish today. Their blankets were longer than wide, usually striped or with zigzag lines. The focal point in the middle of the weaving was usually a serrated diamond.

The Spanish used a horizontal loom of permanent installation. The finished product was a narrow weaving due to the narrow loom. In order to make a wide blanket or rug similar to the Navajo, two panels of the weavings were sewn together down the middle. The yarn used to weave was wool. Vegetal and indigo colors at first were used with commercial dyes used later.

The different manner in which the Rio Grande weavers constructed their blankets and rugs will help you distinguish them from a Navajo or Pueblo blanket or rug. The distinguishing features of the Rio Grande weavings are:

1. The texture is different due to a looser weave.
2. Two identical pieces are usually sewn together lengthwise.
3. The top and bottom of the pieces will have a knotted fringe.
4. At least one double warp in the center of each panel is usually prevalent.
5. The weaving will have a two-ply warp.
6. The weavings will have no borders. Early Navajos have no borders either but the later ones do. The word "Chimayo" is often used to cover all Rio Grande weaving, although actually Chimayo is only a segment of the Rio Grande weaving area. The Rio Grande weavers continued to make weavings into the 1900s.

NON-AMERICAN INDIAN WEAVINGS

A non-American Indian group of weavings that needs mentioning to help the collector distinguish it from others is the Northern Mexican Saltillo. The Saltillo is a blanket or serape that can be identified by its central design of a diamond shape or circular figure on a background of small vertical parallelograms. The blanket or serape will have a narrow border and be woven in two pieces and sewn together down the middle. Saltillos are made of handspun wool with natural and aniline dyes.

The use of a border and the large central design figure usually help distinguish the Saltillo from Rio Grande weavings. Too, the Navajo blanket is considerably different with the main distinguishing factor being that they are made in one piece with no fringe.

THE DEVELOPMENT OF REGIONAL STYLE WEAVINGS

It was during the period that the Navajo were changing from blanket weavers to rug producers in the 1890s at the insistence of the traders that the regional styles of rugs were developed. There are 13 weaving regions that produce a rug characteristic to their region. True, some contemporary rugs today do not fit exactly into a regional style, but they undoubtedly came from one of the regions.

The early white traders are as famous today as the styles they helped to develop. They brought technical as well as artistic form to the art of weaving.

Juan Lorenzo Hubbell of Ganado, Arizona, developed the first regional rug known as the Ganado. The Ganado is a fair-sized rug bordered in black with a dark red background. The uncomplicated designs are in a natural brown, white, gray, and black. There is a central figure, often a diamond or two, which is surrounded by serrations, crosses, zigzags, and other geometric shapes. Finer rugs known as tapestries are also done in the Ganado style.

J.B. Moore was the trader at Crystal, New Mexico, from 1896 to 1911. He was responsible for inspiring the Navajo weavers of his area to make the forerunners of the Tec Nos Pos, Storm Pattern, and the Two Gray Hill rug styles. He wanted bordered, oriental-like designs in handspun natural wool colors. Designs included crosses, diamonds, and a characteristic hook figure that resembles a G on its side. Colors used were red, white, gray, tan, brown, and black.

The original Tec Nos Pos rug has a decorated wide border, and the central pattern is complex with many design elements all outlined in bright contrasting colors.

The Tec Nos Pos Crystal rugs are characterized by three bands of wavy lines or a solid color between complex bands featuring arrows, stars, diamonds, crosses, and other geometric designs.

The Storm Pattern may be the easiest of all to distinguish once you have seen one. The important characteristics are an elaborate rectangle in the middle, four squares in each corner of the rug's design, and lightening bolts connecting the corner boxes to the central box. Colors used are usually gray for the background with designs of red, orange, black, and white.

The Two Gray Hills regional style rug is distinguished by the fact that only natural wood colors of white, black, brown, tan, and gray were used. The border on a Two Gray Hills rug consists of an outer black band, a second border of small geometric figures, and a third border that mirrors the previous border. The central designs are usually elongated diamonds divided and extended by stair-stepped loops and hooks. The blending of different natural colored wool results ·in a variety of subtle shades which makes this rug so collectible.

The Red Mesa style rugs developed 15 miles from Tec Nos Pos. This style is distinguished by its bright, synthetically dyed yarns and the bordered serrated patterns resembling the 19th century Eye Dazzler design.

At Chinle, Arizona, the revival of the Classic style of design was influenced by the efforts of Mary Cabot Wheelwright in the 1920s. This local trader encouraged the weavers to use natural dyes with soft shades of pastel colors and to weave borderless rugs with stripes. What developed was a fine woven rug of pastel colors with stripes of arrows, diamonds, and other small geometric figures. Buyers liked this Chinle revival, and it soon became established. This type of rug was also copied by other traders at Wide Ruins,

Arizona, around 1936 and at Crystal, New Mexico, around 1941. Thus the rug styles known as Wide Ruins and Crystal using pastel colors and bands of designs became known also.

Rugs from Wide Ruins are characterized by earthtones and broad and narrow strips of plain color interspersed with bands of geometric designs and narrower bands with more delicate motifs. The hook design of the early Crystal style often appears in the bands of the Crystal revival rugs.

The Burntwater style came later in the 1970s. This style uses the Two Gray Hills designs with vegetal dyed wools in cool pastel colors and earth-tones to create intricate geometric designs.

Another style called Pine Ridge was developed concurrently with the Chinle revival. It is very similar to the Wide Ruins rugs except for the greater use of green.

In the Gallup, New Mexico, area the small Gallup throw was developed. It was made for use as a chair back or table decoration. It is inexpensive and quite available to collect.

The Yei rug comes out of the Shiprock and Lukachukai Mountain areas of New Mexico and Arizona, respectively. It portrays the *Yeis*, or supernatural beings, who communicate between the Navajo and the gods. The rugs from the Shiprock area have a white or very light background with three to six Yei facing forward. The more elaborate Yei rugs will have a long *Rainbow Goddess* going around three sides of the rug. The colors used are a multitude of bright yarns. If the figures are dancing or shown in profile, they are called *Yeii'bicheii*. The Yei rugs made in the Lukachukai area have black, red, and dark backgrounds and are usually thicker.

Another style rug that is different comes from the Coal Mesa area, southeast of Tuba City, Arizona. Here they weave a "raised-outline rug" where additional wefts are used to raise the outline of the design. Also made in this area are two-faced rugs where each side is a different design.

The collector will find many rugs of the 1900s that do not classify into any regional type. Some weavers were not in a sphere of influence by a particular trader, and some weavers just did not want to conform. A surprising percentage of rugs fall into a nonclassified type and can be found in all Navajo local areas.

Other distinctive type rugs are the Sandpainting, pictorial, two-faced, twill weave, and saddle blanket rugs. I have already mentioned all these types except the twill weave as 1890–1910 type weavings. These weavings were all also made at a later date, and some are still being made today. The twill weave is simply a manipulation of the weft threads to form a weave pattern. (See p. 145 for a more complete description of twill weaving.)

Rug sizes vary from small miniature rugs to gigantic full-room floor size. Shapes can be square, rectangular, and round. Long runner types for hallways were also made.

The Pueblo Indians, except for the Hopis, chose not to make rugs. The Hopis made saddle blankets and rugs for trade. They are not as plentiful as Navajo pieces.

OTHER TYPES OF WEAVINGS

Both the Navajo and Pueblo tribes made women's dresses, mantas, and skirts. Dresses were two rectangular woven pieces tied together at the top corners when worn. A belt or sash was tied around the waist. Pre–1900 dresses are very expensive but collectible. The 1900 Pueblo pieces were made for utilitarian purposes only.

Other weavings made were sashes, kilts, vests, shirts, blouses, leggings, belts, and socks, most of them by Pueblo tribes for utilitarian purposes. Older sashes are particularly collectible.

WEAVING TOOLS, MATERIALS, AND TECHNIQUES

Early American Indians used a simple loom to weave which consisted of two upright planks driven into the ground a few feet apart. Each plank had two slots to which a single loom bar was inserted horizontally. The warps were strung vertically from the loom bar and left dangling at the bottom. The wefts were woven into the vertical warps.

The Navajo and Pueblo Indians used the vertical loom, while the Rio Grande Spanish people used the horizontal loom.

The vertical loom is portable and fairly simple to construct. It consists of an outer wood frame with an inner frame that has a horizontal top and bottom bar from which the warp yarn is strung. Usually 5 to 20 warps per inch are placed on the loom vertically. The size of the weaving is determined by the vertical and horizontal distance between the bars and beams.

Alternating warps are separated by two sticks called heddles, one inserted between the even-numbered warps and the other on the odd-numbered warps. Weaving begins at the bottom, and the weaver creates and executes the design in her mind as she weaves, a unique feat in itself!

Sets of warps are moved back and forth by pushing or pulling on the heddles. A flat wooden stick called a batten is used to separate the groups of warps while the yarn weft is laid down horizontally between the warp groups. As the weft is laid down it is pushed down with a wooden tooth comb. The weaver does not have to complete an entire horizontal line of weft. She will usually do the area she can reach easily and come back later to finish. The lines created between the old work and new finished work are called lazy lines. Design changes are executed by color or weave changes on the wefts. After thousands of wefts are laid and hundreds of hours of work are accomplished, the final product emerges. The finished Navajo weaving has the following:

1. Both the top and the bottom of the weavings are wrapped and tucked back; there is no fringe.
2. The outer edges have a salvage.
3. There can be lazy lines found in the weaving.
4. The corner strings are tied tightly.
5. The tapestry weave is used.
6. Later pieces usually have a border.

The horizontal loom is used by the Spanish to make Rio Grande weavings. This loom is stationary and weaves continuously as the warp yarn continues to feed through it. Therefore, long, narrow sections of woven product are manufactured that have to be cut into smaller weavings. When cut, the warps have to be knotted. This leaves a knotted fringe at the two ends. Due to the narrowness of the weavings, usually two pieces are sewn side by side to make one rug or blanket.

These are the distinguishing characteristics of Rio Grande weavings.

1. Knotted fringes at both ends
2. Usually two pieces sewn together down the middle to make one rug or blanket
3. Texture that is usually loose
4. Corner yarns that are tied loosely
5. No framing border around the design

Wool, the main material for weavings, requires many hours of preparation before the loom is used. The preparation encompasses shearing the sheep, washing and drying the wool, carding (the untangling of wool fibers by use of tooth-surfaced boards), the spinning of the wool to make yarn, and the dying of the yarn. Spinning consists of taking a strip of carded wool with the left hand and twisting it around the sticklike handle of a spindle while manipulating the spindle with the right hand. The rotation of the spindle while pulling on the twisted wool lengthens it out, forming yarn. Repeating the process while pulling, stretching, and jerking the yarn eventually produces a fine yarn. Due to the yarn being held in the left hand while spinning, the homespun yarn has a left-hand twist. Machine-made and Pueblo yarn usually twists to the right.

Dying of the woolen yarn is accomplished after spinning. Until synthetic dyes became available to the weavers, natural wool of white, gray, brown, and black were used with the color of blue added by using indigo (blue dye imported from Spain). Indigo blue is very stable and does not bleed or fade. Red was first made available by the use of unraveled trade cloths called bayeta and saxony.

Bayeta is a red wool fabric that is easy to unravel. It was made in Europe and later in the United States. The early bayeta was dyed red with lac. Later, bayeta was dyed with lac and cochineal. Both dyes are produced from powdered insect carcasses. Later American-made bayeta known as "flannel" was unravelled and woven. It produced a fuzzy yarn. Synthetic dyes were used with flannel after the late 1860s.

Saxony is a fine, three-ply, silky textured yarn produced in Europe and used by the Navajo after 1846. Saxony can be distinguished from three-ply Germantown yarn by its larger diameter.

Synthetic dyes reached the Navajo hands in the late 1800s. It was in the 1920s that vegetal dyes were widely used by the Navajo weavers. In the 1930s new synthetic commercial dyes gave the American Indians colors that were more like vegetal-dyed colors.

The weaving techniques involved in the Southwest are tapestry, twill, two-faced, tufted, and circular weaves.

The tapestry weave is the Navajo's favorite, which I have just described while discussing the vertical loom.

The twill weave is the Pueblo's weave and consists of floating wefts over more than one warp at a time to create a raised pattern of color or texture. Some Navajo saddle blankets were made with the twilled weave. There are three types of twill weave used: the plain forms diagonal floating designs, the herringbone forms zigzag appearing patterns, and the diamond twill forms diamond patterns. The two-faced weave is used to produce a different design on each side of the weaving. This is accomplished by doubling the sets of warfs to four and the sets of wefts to two and then weaving a different design on each side of the rug. Pulled warp or wedge weavings were produced prior to 1900. This weave produced a series of diagonal positions while packing the weft in place.

OTHER WOVEN PIECES

In many parts of the West the first woven pieces were rabbitskin blankets made by cutting rabbit pelts into fine strips. The strips were woven in a simple weave to form a blanket. Some rabbitskin blankets of the late 1800s do exist and are occasionally available to collect.

Pendleton blankets are manufactured at the Pendleton Milling Company in Oregon. Around 1900 the Navajo Indians began using Pendleton blankets which they preferred to their own. Although these fine blankets are not American Indian-made, for historic reasons and for their beauty, old Pendleton blankets have become very collectible and affordable.

The Hudson Bay blanket is also a nice woven blanket being bought by American Indian collectors though it, too, was not made by the American Indian. However, early historical pictures of American Indians show them wearing them. Hudson Bay blankets were also cut up and made into leggings and cuffs and used as a trim on many items of apparel. Many collectors of American Indian artifacts will pass up such pieces, although they are truly as American Indian as good beadwork.

COLLECTING AMERICAN INDIAN WEAVINGS

What is it that impels us to collect American Indian weavings? Although it is probably a combination of many factors that influence the collector to acquire these pieces, the strongest factor is the visual impact that the weaving has upon the viewer.

Knowingly or not, native weavers incorporated into the weaving a feeling of warmth, style, and balance of design. A minimal use of color to express design, space, and contrast, and a fineness of technique were all accomplished on a limited surface. A better-quality weaving will stand out to the viewer and become a fascination for the collector who can look at the same weaving over and over again and see and feel different things at different times.

The collector enjoys knowing that he or she is collecting a craft from an American Indian whose heart and soul went into making a weaving that was created from the raw materials around her.

Weavings can also lend much to the decor of a home or office, thereby making it easy to begin collecting with a few pieces which often leads one into more serious collecting. There are also financial rewards as the market continues to rise on the rarer pieces. The prices paid are the best witness to how serious collectors are about their weaving collection. These are some of the reasons for collecting, although for many it is primarily the enjoyment of and fascination for the weavings themselves.

Noted collectors such as William Randolph Hearst and others have enjoyed collecting American Indian weavings. Today thousands of people throughout the world collect everything from sashes to rugs to fine blankets.

What is nice about collecting weavings is the wide selection of available and affordable weavings from which to choose. There are collectors of Contemporary, Transitional, and Classic Period textile pieces.

Affordability is best in the new artists' work. Classic weavings, though available, are very expensive. Most collectors like to have at least one Classic weaving if possible as they are such masterpieces of the weaving art.

Historic weavings from the Great Lakes and Northwest are hard to find but are occasionally for sale. Hunting for these rare pieces is a challenge.

BUYING, SELLING, AND TRADING

Before jumping into buying expensive textiles, one should study the sources of information available and then gradually start purchasing weavings from the ground up. Of course, select the best quality you can afford. In weavings, knowledge of the fiber used, weave, styles, and age will take time to acquire.

Again, find people in the field that you can trust. This may be a museum curator, a dealer in weavings, an appraiser, or a collector. A buyer needs to have at least two people he or she can show potential purchases to for their input.

Weavings do take up space, so purchase pieces that work into your display and storage arrangements.

Listed here are the main points to consider when purchasing a weaving, specifically rugs, tapestries, and blankets:

1. Be absolutely sure it is American Indian-made and conforms to the proper style of the tribe and area to which it is attributed.
2. Look carefully at the rug. Do not purchase it without laying it out on the floor and examining it. Look at both sides for uniformity, color, design, fineness, and

condition. Straight sides and top and bottom edges are important.

3. Select only the best condition. This is very important. Many textiles are old and worn. Look for color runs (bleeding), broken warps, holes, moth damage, stains, weak spots, and rot. Many rugs and blankets on the market today have been repaired. This is all right as long as the seller informs you, the work is good, and the price is in accordance with its condition.

4. Be sure the design is even and balanced. If the piece is authentic and in suitable condition, then check to be sure vertical and horizontal designs are straight.

5. Determine the fineness of weave. Be sure no warps show through the weaving. The thickness of the rug should be even with no bumpiness or thin spots. Is it the proper weave for the tribe making it?

6. Check the color uniformity. Also, determine if the piece has been redyed. Any bleeding of color (usually red) should be avoided, although that can be removed by the restorers of today. Regarding price to pay, review the market for such pieces and make the best purchase you can. There are enough sales to come up with comparable prices.

Selling your weavings is covered in the opening chapter. Remember, the best pieces resale the best, so buy the best.

You may feel that the very expensive pieces are out of your financial reach, but by trading up one will often be surprised at what can be traded for. Consider trading items for equal or better pieces.

QUALITY IN WEAVINGS

What determines quality in a weaving? The appeal of different weavings is individual, however there are certain criteria for quality that exists in all good weavings. These are:

1. Excellent workmanship including fine weaving.
2. Designs that reach out to the viewer and are balanced.

3. Color and style used properly in relation to the type of piece it is supposed to be.
4. The proper yarn type for the piece, e.g., a Classic Period piece: In the Southwest bayeta, saxony, and indigo blue-dyed natural wool are vital to great masterpieces, while in a Chilkat blanket of the Northwest the yarn must be of mountain goat hair, cedar bark, and sometimes otter fur.

CARING FOR AND DISPLAY OF WEAVINGS

Weavings that are properly cared for will last many years for collectors to enjoy. Smaller weavings such as bags, sashes, and garters can easily be displayed and do not require much room. However, blankets, rugs, mantas, shirts, and larger pieces do require more space. Collectors of many larger pieces should consider a rotation plan to show off their collection, and store pieces to release display stress periodically.

Displaying floor weavings should be done with pads under the full size of the rug. Pads made of rubber or formaldehyde should not be used. As little walking as possible should be done on rugs. A rotation of rugs to less walked-on areas helps. Do not put these collector rugs under planters or metal furniture that can leak onto or rust the rug. Use plastic coasters under furniture placed on top of rugs.

Weavings displayed vertically suffer most from the stress of hanging. One needs to delocalize the points of stress when hanging these rare collectibles.

Be sure to do the following:

1. Hang the weaving in the direction of the warps.
2. Avoid direct light and reduce indoor light to a minimum.
3. Never place the weaving near heaters, air vent, or fireplaces.
4. Use velcro strips sewn to cotton webbing with the webbing sewn to the weaving. The second piece of velcro is placed on a thin board that is attached to the wall.

5. Do not leave a weaving hanging more than three
    months without resting it in storage in order to release
    the stress of display.

Proper temperature and humidity are important. Temperature over 72
degrees and humidity over 55 percent can be detrimental to wool
collectibles. Be sure the storage container is free of insects and is strong
enough so that rodents or pets cannot get into it.

When storing small weavings, lay them down flat on top of each other
with the heaviest on the bottom. Put acid-free paper in between each item.

When storing large weavings, roll the weaving on cardboard rolling tubes
that are covered with polyethylene. The tubes can be obtained at your local
carpet store. Roll the collectible weaving in the direction of the warps and
do not fold. The storage area should be dust-free and no moth balls or crystals
placed with the weavings as moth eradication should be done before storing
(described below). Remove and examine stored collectible weavings
periodically.

Cleaning your weavings is very important. Cleaning should be done by
professionals who understand and work mainly on American Indian
weavings. The method used to clean rugs and blankets consists of vacuuming
and wet and dry cleaning. The only method the collector should use is to
vacuum his or her pieces periodically. Dry cleaning not done by a specialist
in American Indian weavings is considered to be dangerous.

Pest control is very important. The best preventatives are cleanliness and
careful use of moth balls or crystals. Periodic vacuuming removes moth eggs
and larvae from the weavings. Moth balls and crystals should be used by
putting the weaving in a large airtight container with moth balls or crystals
that are in a separate cloth container not touching the weaving.

RESTORATION

There are expert restorers of weavings available. Repairing can be
expensive, so have the restorer give you an estimate prior to doing the work.
Add the cost of the damaged piece to the cost of restoration, and if the total

is less than its market value, it may be worth doing. Inexpensive pieces rarely merit the cost of restoration, although expensive masterpieces, if purchased correctly, will. When contracting for restoration insist upon the following:

1. A firm estimation of the costs
2. The specific length of time to do the work
3. A written guarantee of satisfaction

RECORD KEEPING

Each weaving should have a tag placed at a corner to identify it and to tie it into records kept. Be sure to record the following:

type of weaving	tribe
when made	name of weaver (on newer pieces)
size and description	insurance details

Good photographs and videotapes are recommended in case of loss and as a means to review your collection.

THE WEAVING MARKET

Weavings have been strongly advancing in price for the last 30-40 years. The price of masterpieces such as Classic blankets have set records for American Indian art pieces. The lesser-quality rugs and blankets have not done very well. As in any market, there have been ups and downs, but the trends for the last 100 years have been up.

For the average collector of rugs, a wide price range of collectibles is available. Prices on 1920–1940 rugs range from $150 to thousands of dollars.

The collectibility of Great Lakes and Prairie sashes and bags is limited, however fine woven sashes periodically turn up for sale at moderate prices.

The Northwest Chilkat blanket is very expensive and availability is limited. Figure on a price tag of at least $30,000 for an old Chilkat blanket.

With the strong upsurge in prices, some investors have been in the market, but weavings, like other American Indian art pieces, are mainly sought after by the true lover of American Indian art.

Although a Classic First Phase Chief's blanket may fetch nearly $500,000, a Classic Third Phase Chief's blanket $25,000-$175,000, and a Classic Serape $20,000-$100,000, do not let these prices scare you away. There are hundreds of beautiful native weavings available to collect at very reasonable prices.

Appraising your weaving collection is a must. Knowing the open market value is pertinent to sell, trade, insure, or donate. Too often one thinks that he or she is up on the market when changes have taken place that even everyday traders have trouble keeping up with.

With the cost of appraising still at very low levels, a collector should have his or her collection professionally appraised. Usually the fee is a flat fee and rarely exceeds one percent of the piece's value.

For buying, selling, or trading, knowing your collection's open market value puts you on equal ground with the buyers, dealers, and auctioneers.

REPRODUCTIONS

Yes, there are plenty of weavings that are reproductions and made to look a lot like American Indian weavings.

The major area of confusion I have encountered is with the Mexican look-a-like rug that has the same patterns as the Navajo, is made of wool wefts, and sells for only about 20 percent of a Navajo's value. The Mexican weavers create fine-looking weavings, but upon examination of the weaving process, you can tell the difference between the two.

However, despite the fact that the Mexican rug looks very much like the Navajo, there are three distinct ways to tell Mexican rugs apart from Navajo ones:

1. The Mexican rug has no salvage yarn woven down the outside edges.
2. The are no lazy lines.
3. The outer warp of the Mexican rug is double or heavier that the single outer warp of the Navajo.

Unfortunately, there are unscrupulous sellers who label and sell these reproductions as "handwoven," "Indian," or "Pueblo," etc., without telling the buyer that they are actually Mexican rugs.

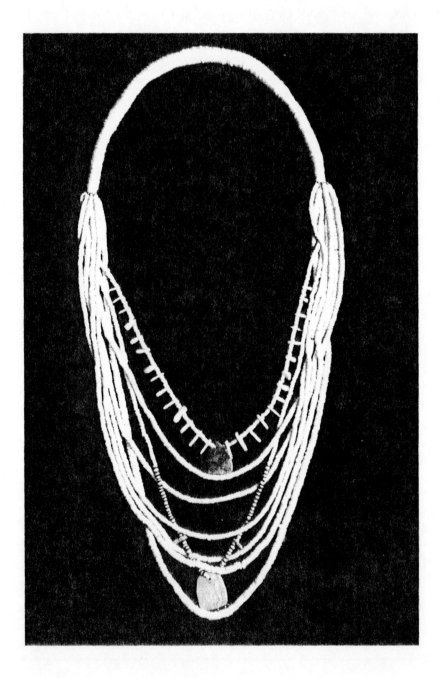

Prehistoric Anasazi necklace (restrung)

7

AMERICAN INDIAN JEWELRY

HISTORY

American Indians have been making and wearing jewelry since their arrival on the North American continent. Jewelry items have always been a means to decorate the body and were used as a symbol of status.

All tribes made some form of jewelry, however the main groups covered in this chapter are the Northwest, Plains, and Southwest tribes.

What is unique about American Indian jewelry is that each tribe involved in its making has created a distinct traditional style. Also unique is how recent it's been since some of the jewelry styles evolved, with metal jewelry being the most recent.

PREHISTORIC JEWELRY

Most prehistoric jewelry has disintegrated except for stone, bone, native copper, horn, ivory, teeth, and shell. The beautiful wood, feather, and seed decorative items made by the prehistoric people can rarely be collected.

Throughout North America early man used many natural products to make beads, pendants, gorgets, ear ornaments, lip labrets, nose plugs, rings, mosaic buckles, bracelets, and fetishes.

The Southeast and Midwest tribes used native copper to make elaborate and delicate ornaments such as pendants, badges, breastplates, gorgets, ear spools, and head and hair ornaments. Native copper was mined by the American Indians near Lake Superior in what is known as the Old Copper Culture area. Copper was used in the Great Lakes and traded to the Southern, Eastern, and Midwest tribes.

The Northwest tribes made jewelry out of dentalium shell, wolf teeth, sea lion teeth, sea otter teeth, whalebone, whale baleen, ivory, seal teeth, stone, bone, and horn. They made pendants, beads, rings, necklaces, nose rings, bracelets, lip labrets, charms, combs, and blanket pins.

The Eskimo of the Far North had whale baleen, animal teeth and bone, stone, and ivory (some of it fossilized) to manufacture lip labrets, pendants, earrings, wrist guards, buttons, necklaces, combs, and charms.

Of all the Prehistoric American Indians, the Anasazi, Mogollon, and Hohokam of the Southwest were the most prolific quality jewelry makers. Due to the many prehistoric jewelry pieces that have been found in the Southwest, the collector has a chance to build a quality collection.

The shell jewelry carvings of the Arizona Hohokam (circa 300–1250 CE) is unsurpassed in fine detail and craftsmanship. Beautiful animal fetishes, carved bracelets, ornate zoomorphic pendants, mosaic-covered shell, and carved shell rings are but a few of the pieces made by these masters of the shell.

Stone, bone, horn, and wood were also masterfully used by the Prehistoric Southwest tribes. Turquoise stone was made into pendants, mosaic units, and fetishes. Red hematite and black jet was available and worked into jewelry. Pyrite mirrors, sandstone plaques, etched bone, shell, and decorated hairpins are but a few examples of their fine workmanship.

Tiny beads smaller than the head of a pin were made by the Southwest tribes, drilled with a cactus needle, and strung into necklaces. These were but a few of the millions of beads made of all the materials available.

The Anasazi were fantastic jewelers also. From 300 CE–1600 CE they artistically designed stone, shell, bone, and horn beads. Fine stone-drilled tabs, pendants, fetishes, and rings were used daily by the Anasazi. Very small stone beads strung into fancy necklaces have been found and collected.

Mosaic inlay of small square units of turquoise, jet, and hematite are often found associated with finely carved shell frogs, discs, and pendants. Mosaic was also inlaid on wood, bone, and stone backing. These are beautiful collectibles, rare and hard to find but exquisite beyond description.

Meanwhile, the Mimbres Culture in Southern New Mexico were also making fine prehistoric jewelry. Most of the pieces described for the Anasazi were also made by this Mogollon Culture.

The early California tribes lavished themselves with jewelry made from abalone shell, seeds, stone, bone, and horn. Probably the finest abalone shell pendants come from the early California and Oregon tribes. Cut, etched, and drilled, these shell pendants are very collectible and reasonably priced. Necklaces, rings, pendants, shell disc beads, charms, earrings, lip labrets, and bracelets were also made by the California and Oregon tribes.

HISTORIC JEWELRY

During historic times the American Indians started making jewelry from trade items as well as the materials used during prehistoric times. The American Indians were very fond of the glass beads, bone, shell, metal, and manufactured items obtainable by trade with European traders. Now the American Indians could add color to their jewelry pieces.

Midwest and Eastern tribes traded for wampum shell beads made for them as well as other manufactured items. Eventually European traders made glass wampum beads in white and purple colors and traded them to the American Indian. Wire, lead, files, kettle metal, brass discs, and glass beads became quite available in the early 1700s. Also, silver gorgets, brooches, and bands were made by silversmiths for trade to the American Indians. Eventually, cheaper metals such as zinc, German silver, and copper took over the demand.

The Plains tribes welcomed glass beads, metals, and pre-made jewelry items. In the mid–1800s German silver was brought to the tribes at which time they began to make brooches, bracelets, conchos, combs, earrings, headbands, rings, hair ornaments, crosses, beads, and horse bridles. The

Plains Indians decorated the German silver by engraving and filing. They also learned to use copper, brass, silver, and tin.

In the Northwest, North, and West Coast the introduction of faceted glass beads by Russian trading posts was welcomed by the American Indian tribes, as it added color to their jewelry. As in the other culture areas, metals were also introduced such as copper, brass, and silver along with other colorful beads. The Haida were making some jewelry pieces from black argillite as well as gold and silver.

In the Southwest, during the mid–1800s the Navajo watched the Mexican craftsman make jewelry and horse gear from iron, brass, copper, and silver. While incarcerated at Bosque Redondo from 1863 to 1868, the Navajo learned some of the techniques of metalsmithing. After returning to their native lands the Navajo began to make silver jewelry.

The Navajo were inspired both by the Plains Indian jewelry and the Spanish Culture European-style jewelry. They saw metal crosses, copper bells, metal jinglers, buttons, iron buckles, gorgets, pendants, horse bits, and bridles being made. From this environment was born the style and tradition of Southwest Navajo silver jewelry. Like many other tribes, the Navajo believed that jewelry was a symbol of status. By 1880 silver jewelry production had increased as the other Pueblos bought or traded for this jewelry. About this same time Navajo silversmiths taught the Zuni people the art of silversmithing. Later, in the mid–1800s, the Zuni passed this knowledge on to the Hopi people.

Each tribe has developed their own style of jewelry. Many Navajo specialized in silver jewelry and turquoise stones set in silver. The Zuni made beautiful inlay accomplished with many small stones including turquoise, while the Hopi worked mainly with metal and small stones.

At first silver was very hard to acquire, so the Navajo used silver from the coins of Mexico and the United States. These were melted into ingots and pounded into sheets.

TECHNIQUES OF DESIGN

The techniques to put designs on metal jewelry came in this order: filing, engraving, chisel marking, repoussé, stamping, and embossing. The early pieces are simple with simple designs.

Annealing and soldering were learned by 1870, and the casting process using tufa stones as molds was accomplished about this time.

Early silversmiths used filing, chasing, and engraving to accomplish their designs. Simple stamping was also used to add a third dimension to their work.

By 1890 turquoise stones began to be set in silver. Little did the artists know then that they were starting a very large commercial enterprise.

To the Southwest American Indians, turquoise possesses religious and magical qualities. Its beautiful blue color reminds them of the big, blue, open sky. Its application to their jewelry is inevitable.

Today's turquoise is treated, and it is an accepted practice to preserve the blue color. The stones used in old jewelry were untreated and therefore greenish hues were evident.

Coral is considered to be an ornament of great power by Southwest Indians. Supposedly its power can cure illness and the wearer of coral will have good luck and virility.

NAVAJO JEWELRY

By 1910 the First Phase (1860–1910) of Southwest jewelry making— which did not include stone work of any kind and with brass as one of the major metals used—came to a close with the Second Phase (1910–1940), a transitional period. During this time the tourist trade flourished to the point where a better name for this period might be the "Commercial Phase" of Southwest jewelry. Many new artists adopted jewelry making as a business, and due to the pressure for tourist-type jewelry, quality was sacrificed, and much of the traditional designs and forms were lost. Toward the end of this phase the situation was corrected.

The last phase from 1940 until the present saw the improvement of jewelry making taking place due to public education of and competition among the jewelry artists for excellence in design and workmanship. The use of gold, silver, brass, and precious stones added to the beauty and workmanship of the more contemporary jewelry. From this phase were born many top quality artists.

ZUNI JEWELRY

After the Navajo passed the art of jewelry making on to the Zuni in the 1880s, the Zuni developed a style all their own. By 1890 they were setting stone in silver. Turquoise is important to the Zuni in their religion and mythology, so it was natural for them to incorporate it into their jewelry. Zuni jewelry started to show many turquoise stones arranged together (mosaic), and by 1910 the blue stone had taken over. Also in 1910 Zuni earrings of the dangling and tinkling style came about.

The mosaic work of the Zuni is a modern version of their ancient ancestors' mosaic work. Red spiny oyster, turquoise, and black cannel coal sized into tiny pieces are set in a pattern on a single backing. Fancy mosaic work includes beautiful *Sun, Knife Wing,* and *Rainbow Gods* done on bracelets, rings, necklace bolos, and many other fine jewelry pieces.

HOPI JEWELRY

About the mid–1890s, the Hopi of Northern Arizona learned to make silver jewelry. A Zuni smith named Leaned worked silver at the Hopi Reservation where the Hopi watched him until they could do the work themselves.

The first pieces made were indistinguishable from Navajo or Zuni work. However, the Hopi became experts at making silver jewelry pieces with their own style, known as overlay metal work. Overlay jewelry is made by soldering a sheet of metal to a second sheet of metal of the same size that has cut-out designs on it. The two pieces are then oxidized together, and the top piece with the cutouts is polished until it is bright and satiny. The dark areas of the back sheet remain dark, giving the pieces a contrast between the polished area and the background. The Hopi also learned to do cutout-type jewelry as a product of overlay work.

Hopi designs of curved lines in finely balanced layouts are very moving. Accompanying the curved lines are straight and right-angled ones. Later pieces are often animals in stylized forms. Stamping, stonework, and appliqué of wire are sometimes used.

All the general forms of American Indian jewelry were made from belts to necklaces.

OTHER JEWELRY-MAKING AREAS

There was very little jewelry made by other Southwest Indian cultures, although it is known that silversmiths existed at the Isleta, Acoma, Laguna, and the Santa Clara Pueblos in the late 1800s. At Santo Domingo they were masters at making shell, coral, and turquoise jewelry that is sliced and set side by side in a mosaic technique. They also made shell and turquoise beads for use in the making of necklaces and earrings.

Meanwhile, in the North the Eskimos were making ivory, stone, bone, horn, glass beads, and metal items of jewelry. Etched ivory neck collars, beaded clusters of colored glass, stone and ivory labrets, pendants, ivory wrist guards, and bracelets are some of the jewelry items they made in the 1700–1800 period.

Northwest tribes were artists in making carved bone and ivory jewelry. As the Russian trade items came into circulation, beads were used as well as metal and other materials useful in making jewelry.

Northwest jewelry consists of gold and silver bracelets, pendants, brooches, earrings, and cuff links. Also some argillite stone jewelry pieces were made by the Haidas. However, the most popular is the silver and gold bracelets of the Haida. The metal surface is engraved with a crest and the background is cross-hatched or plain. A number of well-known Northwest artists are presently making jewelry. Availability is good at moderate prices.

The Athabascans made beautiful necklaces of dentalium shell, quilled hide bracelets, and other forms of jewelry. They made fewer jewelry items, and to collect them is difficult. The Athabascans did, however, make elaborate necklaces of dentalium shell and glass beads, quilled jewelry, and other pieces.

There are a number of American Indian artists from the Southeast and Southern Plains area who made jewelry out of metal. These items are stickpins, earrings, neckerchief slides, belt drops, roach spreaders, bracelets, arm bands, blouse pins, head combs, hair ornaments, belt buckles, rings, chokers, crosses, breastplates, belts, and necklaces. The American Indian cultures involved are the Sauk and Fox, Pawnee, Koasati, Kickapoo, Arapaho, Comanche, Kiowa, Chitimacha, and Cheyenne. Their method of construction involves usage of German silver sheets cut to the shape desired. Surface embellishment is accomplished by filing, engraving, stamping, and piercing. Some soldering overlay and stone work is incorporated into the German silver work.

TYPES OF SOUTHWEST JEWELRY MADE

From the historic period to the present these are the pieces of jewelry made:

Belts. Concho belts are considered to be the finest pieces of American Indian jewelry. The earliest concho belts (1870–1890) were round or oval with open centers to run the belt through. Design work on each concho was a series of pierced holes encircling the outer edge with stamped designs around the hole. A raised band encircled these stamped designs leaving most of the concho plain.

After 1890 the open center was replaced by closing the belt-fastening hole. The belt was now attached to the concho by copper bands on the back of each concho. This closed-center style continues through today. Buckles for these belts were added about 1900, as were some vertical butterfly plaques. Around the turn of the century turquoise settings were incorporated into the concho. After 1920 sizes and shapes varied due to tourist demand. Normal size concho belts have 6 to 8 conchos.

Bracelets. Early bracelets were of twisted combined wire. From 1880 bracelets were set with stones, and designs were filed and chiseled on. Flat silver bands were also made in these early years and decorated by stamping with repoussé. Repoussé is relief design work on a flat surface where the pattern is raised from the reverse side. Early casted bracelets were also made that appear delicate with straight and curved thin lines in open design. Cast jewelry later became thicker with more curvilinear lines.

As time went on the narrow silver band bracelets became wider with more elaborate designs. The setting of turquoise on these wide bands became popular. During the Fred Harvey retail store years (early 1900s to the mid–1950s), elaborately stamped silver bands with crosses, arrows, whirling logs, thunderbirds, and other elements were made for him to sell to the tourist. These bracelets are very collectible.

Buttons. Silver buttons were an integral part of the American Indian decorative scheme. You will see them used on blouses, medicine bags, shirts, and cuffs. Made from small coins and silver discs, they were decorated by chiseling, stamping, filing, and repoussage. To the back of each button a loop of wire was soldered enabling it to be sewn onto hide or cloth. After 1870 some buttons were made by casting. Other shapes later included butterfly, square, and oval.

Necklaces. The earliest necklaces were simple strands of silver beads. The first additions to the silver necklaces were silver najas. Najas were ornaments the Spanish hung on their horses' bridles. Of course, other items were eventually added to these simple necklaces, such as crosses, squash blossom heads, and coins. The double-barred cross with a heart-shaped bottom was a popular type. In the early 1900s silver coins were put on shanks to form necklaces combined with round silver beads. Coral bead necklaces in the later 1800s were very popular. Turquoise and other stones worked their way into necklace settings, and by the 1920s necklaces were heavy with turquoise.

Pins. Pins are dress ornaments. The early Navajo pieces were simple silver decorated pieces. Later pins were turquoise clusters. Hopi, Zuni, Cochiti, and Santo Domingo Pueblo Indians made interesting pins, too. From the 1930s to 1940s elaborate, large cluster turquoise pins were commonly worn on velvet dresses by the Navajo women.

Rings. Around 1860 the Navajo made their own wire rings, and by 1880 they set single stones in them. Other Southwest tribes also made simple early rings. Larger stones came into use about 1900. The turquoise cluster and large stone rings remain popular. There are a vast amount of rings available in the marketplace.

COLLECTING AMERICAN INDIAN JEWELRY

Collecting American Indian jewelry is unique because it is an American-originated collectible, a recent American Indian art form, and can be displayed by wearing.

The types of jewelry are:

1. general
2. old silver
3. one of a kind
4. turquoise
5. artists' pieces

Seeking out collectible jewelry is easier than most American Indian collectibles, as thousands of pieces are available to be purchased and worn. A visit to most antique stores and you will find the pieces you desire. Otherwise, there are the usual places to purchase jewelry such as Indian stores, galleries, auctions, dealers, jewelry artists, and shows. The earliest silver jewelry is considerably harder to find and collect.

Like any other American Indian relic, jewelry can be purchased, sold, and traded best when people involved are knowledgeable and reliable. Buying old silver from a reputable dealer, gallery, collector, or auction is important, as determining age of old silver is difficult.

Select first the piece that makes you happy. Second, be sure it is North American Indian-made and the workmanship is the best you can afford. Also, select only jewelry made with the correct type stone and metal.

There are thousands of run-of-the-mill-type jewelry pieces on the market, so your careful selection of the better pieces is important. Selling jewelry from your collection can be difficult unless they are the better pieces. Poor-quality pieces will not escalate much in price and cannot be resold for more than one-third of the retail value, while better-quality jewelry will escalate in value.

Your solution is to be sure to buy right on the poorer-quality pieces if this is what you must buy. The top-quality, well-known artist, and the early 1900s silver jewelry pieces will escalate in price and will not be heavily discounted upon your decision to sell.

So, to determine quality do the following:

1. Be sure the work is traditional to the tribe to which it is attributed.
2. Check the stone, shell, horn, ivory, bone, and/or metal used.
3. Examine workmanship for balance, fineness, and execution of work.
4. Check the condition, and also determine if any repair work has been done.

CARING FOR YOUR COLLECTION

Caring for jewelry is simple compared to perishable collectibles such as baskets. Basically, store your jewelry in a safe place and do not clean it or remove the old patina from the silver pieces unless it is so dark as to reduce its value. A soft cloth to wipe off the dust is all you need.

Flat display cabinets are commonly used to display flat-laying jewelry. However, the best display method is wearing your jewelry.

Repairing your pieces should be done only by an experienced American Indian jeweler. Check your dealer for names of repair people. Often at Indian shows there are jewelers who do repairs on the premises.

Keeping good records of your American Indian jewelry is important. Also insuring it and knowing its current market value is necessary. When appraising your collection, find an appraiser that either deals, collects, or is very much involved with the everyday market of American Indian jewelry.

THE MARKET FOR AMERICAN INDIAN JEWELRY

The present market is steady with good demand for quality pieces. Early 1900s silver jewelry is always in good demand and the prices are firm.

Remember, the true value of American Indian jewelry is derived from the artistry and not from the amount of stone or metal used.

Often American Indians traded or paid debts with their jewelry. The American Indians of the Southwest sometimes used their jewelry to borrow money at the local trading post. Some people call the jewelry that was not redeemed from the trading post "Old Pawn." Actually, Old Pawn is American Indian jewelry that has been owned, pawned or not. Collecting Old Pawn is fun and the supply is large.

Today there are laws to try to curb non-American Indian-made pieces from being represented as American Indian-made when they are not. The State of New Mexico has such a law on the books. These laws were written to protect both the American Indians and the consumer from misrepresentation of nonauthentic jewelry.

8

STONE, BONE, HORN, SHELL, AND IVORY COLLECTIBLES

HISTORY

Most collectors remember their first contact with an American Indian arrowhead or stone artifact. A boy scout on a camp stumbles upon an arrowhead along the trail, a Midwest farm girl finds at her feet in a plowed field an object of an ancient American Indian, a Northwest fisherman chances upon a worked stone artifact along the edge of a river, a Southwest cotton farmer plows up a stone figure in his cotton field. These are but a few examples of collectors' fond memories of their first finds that may have started them on the fun experience of collecting American Indian artifacts. Finding an artifact that has not been touched by another human hand for hundreds of years is overwhelming to say the least. Searching out and collecting bone, horn, shell, and ivory artifacts is just as exciting. These collectibles (which span the years from 4000–9000 BCE to recent times) consist of tools, weaponry, jewelry, ceremonial items, and objects used in food preparation and housekeeping, and in hunting, fishing, and games.

The fun of collecting stone, bone, horn, shell, and ivory artifacts comes not only from our early experiences with them, but from the plentifulness of them. All areas of North America have been lived in by Early Man and American Indians at one time or another, so it's not surprising that their

Prehistoric jewelry of bone and stone

stone tools and arrows have been found and are still being found almost everywhere. The great variety of types, styles, and usage of these items stimulate the collector to want one or more of each.

To categorize stone artifacts, I have divided them into two major groups. First, there are the flinted stone pieces, and second, the picked, abraded, and polished stone artifacts. The flinted artifacts consist of projectile points, knives, scrapers, drills, reamers, punches, hoes, axes, and gravers. The second category consists of stone bowls, axeheads, adzes, chisels, gouges, picks, mauls, manos, pestles, shaft straighteners, abraders, polishers, bannerstones, effigies, gorgets, fetishes, pendants, plummets, game balls, and pipes.

Flinted projectile points and knives are the most commonly collected stone artifacts. They are found in almost all areas of the United States. An arrowhead is the head of a shafted arrow used to hunt game and fight enemies. Early spearheads were used on atlatls and shafted spears. Wherever American Indians hunted or fought they lost arrows, knives, and spearheads; that is why we still find these pieces today.

Chipped or flinted artifacts were made from good quality rock material that could be worked by chipping. The type of rock varied by geographic area, but in all cases the highest quality of stone was desired by the flinter so that he could control the flaking. Quality gemstone for making projectiles consists of jasper, agate, quartz, petrified wood, opal, jade, chalcedony, and cherts. Various types of flint were used to make most of the Midwest and Eastern projectile points.

METHODS OF MANUFACTURE

Flinting was the method used to make these chipped artifacts. Flinting consists of selecting a stone that will fracture predictably when struck (percussion method) or pressure-flaked (removal of small pieces by pressure).

A large core rock is selected for its quality of flinting, then it is struck with a harder rock. Large flakes come off that can be made into flinted artifacts. The cored flake is then shaped by striking it with pieces of harder rock (hammerstone) or a large dense piece of horn. When the shape is satisfactory to the flinter, the edges are usually sharpened and made even with the use of a horn to pressure off small flakes. This whole process is not as cumbersome or time-consuming as one would think. It is said that an American Indian could make a good arrowhead in the field in 3 to 5 minutes. Of course, more elaborate pieces took longer.

To aid in chipping a piece of rock more easily, the stone was sometimes heated. This process involved heating the core rock up to a high temperature then allowing it to cool. This changed the molecular structure which made the fracturing easier and more predictable.

The technique of flinting has been mastered by modern man and is even taught in some colleges. It is a very relaxing hobby. Most modern flinters enjoy their hobby and do not sell their product as of old. However, unscrupulous owners often try to pass off well-made replicas of pieces as old and authentically American Indian-made. This has hurt some collectors' desires to purchase flinted artifacts. It has also stimulated collectors and dealers to examine the pieces they purchase very closely. Unfortunately, there is a large amount of reproductions out there in the marketplace.

TIME PERIODS OF PROJECTILE POINTS AND SPEARS

The time periods for stone arrowheads, spearheads, and knives follow. Since there are price and identification guides for specific flint projectile points and knives, I have listed only the more popular ones collected.

Paleo Period (4000–9000 BCE)

Clovis	Eden
Cumberland	Dalton
Folsom	Meserve
Plainview	Pinto Basin
Agate Basin	Sandia
Redstone	Angostura
Scottsbluff	Big Sandy

Archaic Period

Oldest (9000–7000 BCE)

Calf Creek	Nebo Hill
Crump Lake	Pine Tree
Dovetail	Sedalia
Eva	Thebes

Middle (7000–4000 BCE)

Hardin	Kirk
Lost Lake	Benton
Buzzard Roast Creek	Carrizo
Crescent	Langtry
Montrell	Pedernales
Pickwick	Uvalde

Later (4000–3000 BCE)

Adena	Etley
Motley	St. Charles
Turkey Trail	Wade

Later Prehistoric record (3000–1600 BCE)

Dickson	Gibson
Alba	Hopewell Corner Notch
Agee	Jacks Reef
Cahokia	Darl
Ocala Perdez	Duval
Snyder	Deadman

There are hundreds of projectile points that are not classified in this book but are still nice to collect—especially if you have found one yourself.

WESTERN PROJECTILE POINTS AND SPEARS

Since the Western points are not usually as well covered as those in other areas, I will discuss with you in more detail the major collectible points from the Western states of Washington and Oregon, California, Arizona and New Mexico, Nevada, Utah, Idaho, Wyoming, Montana, and Colorado.

Washington and Oregon have some of the finest gem points ever to be found and collected in the world. Due to the glacial movement through the Columbia River gorge millions of years ago, large fields of agate, jasper, quartz, and other gemstones were exposed. The American Indians refined these gemstones to arrowheads, atlatl points, spears, drills, and knives. Since many tribes occupied the area for centuries, thousands of points were made and left there. In addition to the Columbia River area, Oregon's Warner Valley has produced remarkable points for the collector. This valley, the high desert area around Fort Rock, and Christmas Valley were American Indian strongholds, and some collectors have found nice flinted pieces in these areas. As one moves south into Oregon, the stone points found will be more obsidian and less gemstone. Oregon has many obsidian quarries that the Indian flinters used. The Rogue River in Oregon has presented the collector with the most graceful fine-flinted fish points to be found—the Rogue River point. Here the stones used were jasper, quartz, agate, obsidian, and other quality stones. The Washington state line lies on the Columbia River for many miles, and fine points are found near the river and into various parts of the state.

California is 1,000 miles long and has close to 100 different American Indian tribes that made thousands of projectile points over a period of a thousand years. Since there are 32 locations in California where good quality obsidian was quarried by American Indians, the majority of points are made of obsidian. Obsidian is a volcanic product created from rhyolite under volcanic heat and pressure. Since obsidian flints easily and can be found in 16 different types, surely the American Indians found it a good source for making points. The main types of obsidian are: black, red, gray, green, blue, translucent, mahogany, snowflake, rainbow, and black-red mix. Many small to large points were made of obsidian, and even large ceremonial dance blades 12 to 30 inches long were made in prehistoric and historic times by the Karok Indians for trade to the Hupa tribe.

Along the Central Coast of California, the American Indians found a brown, black, green, and gray chert that they worked to make projectile points. Since chert is a lower grade of stone for flinting, the points are more crude. Occasionally a very fine piece would develop. Farther into the lower California desert area one will find some obsidian, but more red and white arrowheads appear.

Arizona and New Mexico were homes for thousands of prehistoric people who used atlatls and later bows and arrows. New Mexico is the home of the Clovis point named after Clovis, New Mexico, where it was originally found. The Sandia points were discovered near Sandia, New Mexico.

The Anasazi and Mogollon were responsible for the smaller-type points. Arizona can take credit for the finest serrated ceremonial points known as Hohokam Ceremonial Serrated. One thousand years old, these delicate ceremonial points range from 1 to 4 inches long. Arizona also had the Anasazi who made thousands of small bird-like points and larger spears and knives. Although quality stone for flinting was scarce in the Southwest, obsidian and other quality stone was traded. Petrified wood, however, was plentiful and put to good use by the American Indian flinters.

Farther north in Utah, Montana, Idaho, and Nevada many fine arrowheads, atlatl points, drills, and knives have been collected. Nevada projectile points are primarily obsidian and basalt. The desolate Black Rock Desert in Northwestern Nevada still produces good finds. Some white chert, agate, and jasper points are hunted in Nevada. Idaho has basically the same type of obsidian points, however in Northern Idaho there have been archeological finds of large flinted blades, Clovis, and many other points from early cultures; very few of these large pieces are in collectors' hands. Utah and Montana have a variety of types and colors of Western flinted points. Utah has the Fremont Indian Culture as well as the Anasazi to draw upon for good points.

TYPES OF WESTERN PROJECTILE POINTS AND SPEARS

Listed below are the main types of flinted projectile points, knives, crescents, and blades of the Western United States.

Black Rock Concave Base. A small triangular point with a concave base, usually obsidian.

Ceremonial Dance Blade. these are very large obsidian blades with a long leaflike shape. They run in size from 12 to 30 inches long. They were made by the Karok tribe and traded to the Hupa for their Deer Dance. Ceremonial blades were still being made in the early 1900s.

Chumash Blade. A medium-to-large flinted knife blade that is leaf-shaped with an area on one end for the hafting into a wood handle. Green, red, brown, and black chert was used.

Chumash Leaf Point. A small-to-large size leaf-shaped point made of California coastal chert.

Crescent. A crescent-shaped piece, 1-4 inches long, flinted on both sides. Can be of any type of Western stone. Found in most of the Western states.

Crump Lake. A large short-stemmed point with a thick body. Usually longer than wide, named after Crump Lake, Oregon.

Desert Side Notch. Usually a small point with a concave base and notched at each corner. Found in all the Western states.

Elko. Corner-notched point that is small to medium in size. The stem is very indented and the ears at the corners are thin and sharp. Most Elkos were made from obsidian.

Gunther. This is a triangular-shaped, needlelike point with sides that are straight to concave with a short stem. Workmanship is usually fine. They are found mainly near the Columbia River, however they can be found in other Western states.

Gypsum Cave. An elongated, thin, triangular, medium-size point. It has straight lateral edges, making up most of the point; the back edges slant quickly to a nub for a base. These are found in Nevada and Oregon.

Hohokam Lateral Notch. A small 1-2 inch bird point, triangular, and very thinly made with distinct side notches.

Hohokam Serrated. These are 1-4 inches long, heavily serrated points. Some show a crescent-shaped base, others have straight-edged bases.

STONE, BONE, HORN, SHELL, AND IVORY COLLECTIBLES 175

Humbolt Concave Base. A small to medium point with a concave base. Its sides are leaf-shaped, and the stone used is usually obsidian. These points are found mainly in Oregon and Nevada.

Kalapuyas. A small barbed bird point that has a little contracting stem. Usually found in Oregon.

Klickitat Dagger Point. A dagger-shaped small point with small barbs. Usually made of quality gemstone and found near the Klickitat River on the Columbia River Oregon side.

Leaf Blade. These are large knives shaped like a leaf.

Leaf Point. Medium to large points shaped like a leaf with points on both ends. Usually made of obsidian.

Mad River. A deep corner-notched point with fine flaking usually about 2 inches long. Rarely, one is found with small notches in each ear. They are from Oregon and Northern California.

Mohave Point. A slender lanceolate-shaped point with the broadest part about three quarters up from the base. The upper portion shows edges slightly rounded, while the bottom edges are straight. These are very old points (7000–9000 years) found near the Lake Mohave area of Southeastern California. Similar type points are also found in the Southwest.

Mule-Ear Knife. A Columbia River knife shaped like the ear of a mule, it is medium-sized with a concave broad base that is thinned. The shoulders of this knife are prominent.

Northern Side-Notched. This is a medium-size point with distinct side notches and an incurvate base, usually fine flaking in obsidian and other Western stone. Found in most of the Western states.

Pinto Basin. This is a medium-size point with straight sides. The back end will have a distinct bifurcated stem causing shoulders that go back, are sloping or horizontal. Found mainly in Oregon, Washington, California, and Nevada, and occasionally in other Western states. Primarily made of obsidian and chert.

Rio Grande Point. Medium-size point, lanceolate shape with a contracting stem. These points are found in New Mexico.

Rockwell. This triangular-shaped corner notch is very similar to the Gunther. It is found in Washington, Idaho, Oregon, and California.

Rogue River. A finely chipped, small-to-medium size barbed point. The barbs spread out to the sides of the point. Usually one barb is longer than the others. There are triangular-shaped Rogue River points also. The main location of origin is Oregon, and they are usually made of quality gemstones.

Rose Spring. A small corner-notched point with a blunt stem, found in most Western states.

Schoolhouse. This is a basal-notched, Christmas tree-shaped, medium-size point. Its distinguishing feature is that the stem and both barbs are all squared off evenly. These points are from the Columbia River area.

Stockton Curve. These are serrated points made of obsidian in the form of a bear's claw. Used in ceremonial dances up until the early 1900s.

Stockton Serrated Knife. A large serrated knife made from obsidian.

Stockton Serrated Point. Found in the Sacramento and Stockton River Valleys of California. These points are heavily serrated, medium-size points. Some are notched and some are not. They are almost always made of obsidian.

Wintum. A small serrated point with basal corner notches, usually made of obsidian and found in Northern California.

Yaki. A medium-size point side-notched with a long slender, thin appearance. Both sides are straight, ending in a sharp point. These are usually obsidian from the upper Sacramento Valley of California.

OTHER STONE ARTIFACTS

The following stone collectibles were made by the methods of picking, abrading, and polishing:

Stone bowls. These are round bowls with a hole from the top to partway down.

Usage. Stone bowls called mortars in the West were used for crushing seeds. Crushing is accomplished with the use of a pestle.

Material. The bowls are made of hard stone common to the areas of production.

Size. The size varies from 2-inch miniatures to 24-inch diameter bowls. The average bowl is about 9 inches in diameter and 8 inches tall. The hole in the middle where seeds are placed for grinding varies from 2 inches to as deep as the bowl. Many mortars have been found with holes all the way through them from years of usage.

Areas of origin. West Coast, Northwest, Midwest, and the Northeast

Types. There are hard stone and soft stone (such as steatite) bowls. Most bowls are plain, however bowls from the Northwest and Canada are often carved with effigy and geometric designs.

Collectibility: There are many bowls available at inexpensive prices.

Pestles. A tubular-shaped, worked stone usually round in the cross section.

Usage. Pestles are worked in company with a mortar for grinding seeds by pounding and twisting the pestle in the mortar. In the Northwest they are also used to pack fish.

Material. Hard stone from the area of usage

Size. The length varies from inches to 2-3 feet. The diameter is always small compared to the length.

Areas of origin. West Coast, Northwest, Midwest, and Northeast

Types. Most pestles are very plain, however effigy pestles, phallic-shaped, ringed pestles, conical, bell, and roller pestles are found.

Collectibility. Plain pestles are very common and inexpensive, while effigy pestles are rare and very expensive.

Mauls. A maul is a short, heavy, hard stone tool.

Usage. Mauls were used for driving wedges and stakes. Some were used like pestles to grind seeds or paint in stone mortars.

Size. There are miniatures 2 inches tall and large mauls that can reach as high as 16 inches or more.

Area of Origin. Northwest

Types. There are hand mauls with flat, nippled, or grooved tops. There are also stirrup, cylinder, and perforated mauls.

Collectibility. There are lots of mauls available at moderate to high prices.

Metates and Manos. A metate is a rectangular stone, sometimes very large with a trough area on top. A mano is a round or square rock used to rub on the trough area of the metate to grind seeds.

Material. In the Southwest a dense volcanic rock was usually used for the metate. Other rock types were also found. The manos are usually of a hard stone from the area.

Size. Metates are usually about 1-1/2 feet long and 10 inches wide with a depth of anywhere from 2 inches to as deep as the metate. The largest collected was the size of a bathtub while some miniature ones have been found. Manos are made to fit the metate.

Area of origin. Southwest

Types. The Southwest type has no legs and is rectangular and large. The Mexican type sometimes found in the Southwest has 3 legs, and the Fremont Culture type has a separate trough at the top end of the metate to store the mano. Manos may be round or square.

Collectibility. Metates are very plentiful and inexpensive as are manos.

Plummets. A long tear-shaped stone fully worked and usually polished. It can be drilled, grooved, or made for nonattachment.

Usage. Ceremonial charm stones and possibly used as bolas in some areas. May also have been used as fishing or netting weights.

Material. Plummets were usually made of hard stone from the area of origin, but softer type stone such as steatite was also used.

Size: From 3 to 14 inches long, they are usually 1 to 2-1/2 inches across.

Areas of origin. East, Midwest, and West Coast

Types. There are undrilled, drilled, grooved, ball-shaped, and tear drop, to name a few.

Collectibility. There are many available at good prices. They are an exciting artifact to collect.

Stone Clubs. Clubs are shaped stone pieces usually 2-3 feet long and heavier on one end than the other.

Usage. Clubs were used for warfare, ceremonial purposes, and for killing animals.

Material. Clubs were made of hard stone and were pecked, abraded, and polished.

Size. The length of a club is usually about 18-24 inches long. Some ceremonial miniatures were made.

Areas of origin. East, West Coast, Southwest, Northwest, and the Far North

Types. There are many types and shapes. In the Southeast there is the Monolithic Axe which is more of a club than an axe. In California and Oregon, there is the rare Slave Killer which is an effigy animal stone club. It was said to have been used in ancient times to dispose of noncooperative captives. In the Northwest there are fish clubs, ceremonial, and slave killer club types. Plain stone clubs were probably common to Early Man.

Collectibility. The rare clubs are very hard to collect due to scarcity and price. More common types are easier to collect.

Adze Blades. These are the worked stone bit prehistorically hafted to a wood or stone handle. The adze blade has dissimilar faces—cone concave near the bit end.

Usage. A finishing tool for shaping wood items

Material. Made from fine hard stone

Size. 1-8 inches long; usually small as these pieces are the blade to a finishing tool and do not need to be heavy like an axehead.

Types. There are approximately 20 hard stone types and 2 chipped types. Categories relate to the shape, grooving, fluting, notches, polls, ridges, and type of bit. California has a unique stone-curved adze handle to be used with a stone or metal blade.

Collectibility. Adzes are more rare than celts or axes and often hard to tell from celts. Prices are moderate except for the rarer types.

Arrow Shaft Straighteners, Abraders, and Polishers. These are stone tools made in small rectangular blocks with grooves on top for straightening and working on the wood shafts of arrows and spears.

Materials. The straighteners are made of hard stone from the areas of origin. The abraders are made from a lighter stone with a porous texture. The polishers are made from sandstone and/or a comparable stone.

Areas of origin. East, Northwest, Southwest, West, and Midwest

Types. There are one-, two-, and three-grooved straighteners. The abraders and polishers are single-grooved and used with a one-groove block on top of the wood shaft and one groove on the bottom. Fancy etched straighteners were found but most are plain.

Collectibility. They are available for collection at reasonable prices.

Gouges and Chisels. Long, narrow stone tools made with a sharp edge for gouging and chiseling wood. Chisels have a beveled bit, and gouges have a bit with a concave groove.

Material. These are made of hard stone and occasionally of slate.

Size. Gouges are usually 2-8 inches long and chisels are about 2-10 inches long. Both are long and narrow.

Areas of origin. Gouges are mainly from the Northeastern United States. Chisels are from areas in the Southern United States as well as the Midwest and Northwest.

Types. There are about 12 types of hard stone gouges and 6 types of chisels.

Collectibility. Not many chisels are available nor are there many collectors. Gouges are available and the prices are moderate.

Celts. Fully worked ungrooved axe-shaped tool, round on one end with a bit on the other.

Usage. This tool was used to work wood.

Materials. Hard stone from the area of origin. Hematite was also used.

Size. From 3 to 8 inches long with a narrow width

Areas of origin. Midwest, Northeast, Southeast, Southwest, and Northwest

Types. There are about 20 types including flint types mentioned in the flinting section of this book. Types are identified by the shape, the cross section of the poll, and the types of bits and edges.

Collectibility. Celts are very plentiful. Average pieces are inexpensive while ceremonial and top quality celts can be expensive.

Axeheads. The stoneworking ends of what was once a prehistoric axe or hammer. Axes will have a groove for the hide or cordage strap attachment to the wood handle.

Usage. A tool for pounding and splitting wood, plus the axe was used for many other daily chores as well as for ceremonial purposes.

Material. Because of the way axes were used, a hard stone is necessary. Each area of origin has used various hard stones including some very unusual and beautiful ones such as porphyry and hematite.

Sizes. Most axeheads are about 6-8 inches long, however there are miniatures and jumbo axeheads. The larger axeheads are more desirable to collectors.

Areas of origin. The Midwest produced some of the finest and rarest pieces. The Southwest also made axeheads as did the Northwest and the East Coast area. An occasional axehead is found in most other areas.

Types. Axeheads are classified by the type of grooves banding the body of the piece. There are full-grooved, three-quarter-grooved, and half-grooved axes. In Wisconsin, there is the fluted axe and in Michigan the barbed axe. Special quality axeheads are called trophy axes.

Collectibility. Axeheads are the stone collector's most favored pieces after flinted points. There were many thousands of axes made and availability is good. Prices run from very inexpensive to very expensive.

Spuds. Long celt with flared blade at one end.

Usage. Primarily used ceremonially. Some were used to dig the soil.

Material. They were made of flint, chert, and other hard stones.

Size. They range in size from 5 to 15 inches.

Areas of origin. Spuds are found in the South, Southeast, and the Midwest.

Types. Most are flinted spuds, but there are spuds of hard stone such as rectangular shaft, tri-edged, fluted, and tapered shaft.

Collectibility. Spuds, though rare, are collectible and prices are moderate to expensive.

Spatulas. Also called spatulates, these have long, narrow, round handles expanding into a blade on one end and tapering to a pole on the other.

Usage. Ceremonial as well as used for digging up roots.

Material. Spatulas are made of hard stone and slate.

Size. They range from 3 to 25 inches long.

Areas of origin. Found in the South, Southeast, and Midwest

Types. There are a half dozen types. Examples you might locate are the perforated slate short forms, square poll, and ceremonial spatulas.

Collectibility. Authentic spatulas are not plentiful.

Game balls. These are rocks that have been made into near-perfect round balls.

Usage. For playing games

Materials. Usually made of hard stone

Size. From 1 to 10 inches in diameter

Areas of origin. Found in almost all areas

Types. All the same except for size

Collectibility. Most collectors overlook the game balls. There are usually a few on the market at very reasonable prices.

Stone Pipes. These are pipes for smoking tobacco.

Material. Most soft stones such as steatite or pipestone; these stones are soft and easily carved when wet, but quite hard when dry.

Sizes. Pipes are found from 1 to 10 inches.

Areas of origin. Almost all American Indians used pipes.

Types. The earliest were tube and ceremonial pipes; later T-bowl pipes were made.

Collectibility. The authentic rare animal effigy pipe is hard to purchase due to scarcity and cost. Most tube pipes are available at moderate prices. Small prehistoric pipes are available and not badly priced, although Plains and Eastern American Indian historic catlinite pipes are available at fairly expensive prices.

Bannerstones. These are beautifully refined stone artifacts that are symmetrical with a drilled hole or notches.

Usage. The usage has been disputed for years; may have been used for ceremonial purposes or as atlatl weights.

Material. The most common material is banded slate. Other stone materials are ferruginous quartz, granite, calcite, limestone, sandstone, hematite, diorite, and steatite.

Size. They range from 3 to 5 inches wide and 2 to 5 inches long.

Areas of origin. Bannerstones have been found in the Midwest, Northeast, and in the South.

Types. There are 32 types of which 2/3 are bifaced and 1/3 are single faces. They are usually named after their shape such as winged, hourglass, humped, reel, crescent, triangular-barreled, shield, tubular, fluted ball, bottled, geniculite, axe, and hinged, to name a few.

Collectibility. They are very collectible. The greater pieces will be hard to secure and prices are fairly expensive.

Birdstones. A bird made of stone with a flat bottom that has one drilled hole in the front and one in the back.

Usage. No one knows for sure, but birdstones were probably used as an atlatl weight.

Material. Slate, porphyry, and hard stone

Size. Average size is 1-1/2 inches wide by 4-1/2 inches long.

Areas of origin. Midwest and Northeast

Types. Popeye, bar, and bust are a few of the types of birdstones.

Collectibility. Birdstones are considered to be one of the best of the stone collectibles. Prices are in the higher ranges, but availability is there if one wishes to pay the price. Many fake pieces do exist.

Gorgets. Flat stone ornaments usually drilled for attachment in 2 or 3 places.

Usage. These were used as a personal adornment and possibly for atlatl weights.

Material. Usually made of slate, but hard stone gorgets do exist.

Size. Average size is 2-4 inches long.

Areas of origin. The Midwest, South, and East are the main areas, but most all areas had some sort of gorget.

Types. There are numerous types. Some are classified as rectangular, expanded centers, boat-shaped, biconcave, quadriconcave, reel-shaped, round, square, and bar.

Collectibility. There is a wide selection of gorgets, as almost all areas made some sort of one. The slate gorgets are highly collectible.

Discoidals. A disc-shaped stone usually hollowed out in the center on both sides although not all the way through.

Usage. A game stone

Material. Usually of granite, quartz, diorite, and many other hard stones. Soft stone such as steatite was sometimes used.

Size. From miniatures of 1-1/2 inches in diameter to larger ones of 4 inches in diameter

Areas of origin. Found mainly in the Midwest down into the South

Types. There are numerous types; a few are named Biscuit, Cahokia, and Jersey Bluff.

Collectibility. Discoidals are very desirable collectibles and can still be found at reasonable prices.

Listed below are other American Indian stone collectibles.

abrading stones	donut stones	picks
anchor stones	earplugs	pile drives
anvils	game stones	prayer sticks
atlatl weights	hammerstones	reamers
bark shredders	hoes	sandal lasts
beads	jewelry items	saws
boatstones	labrets	scrapers
bola stones	medicine tubes	sinker stones
censors	net weights	skipping stones
cogstones	nose plugs	stone cups
cones	nutcrackers	stone effigies
crushers	paint cups	stone fetishes
cup stones	paint pallets	stone markers
digging sticks	pendants	stone whorls

BONE ARTIFACTS

American Indians never wasted any by-products of the animals they killed for food. Bone is one of those products that provided a hard, strong substance from which weapons, tools, and jewelry pieces could be made. Unfortunately, bone does not survive as well as stone, and many artifacts deteriorated before being discovered.

Awls. Long slender bone pieces with a sharp end to pierce leather or baskets in construction of clothing or baskets.

Clubs. For warfare, hunting, and fishing

Combs. Bone combs were used by the Eskimos and other tribes for combing their hair.

Hoes. The shoulder blades of buffaloes were used by the Plains Indians for digging.

Knives. For cutting meat, vegetable products, and for warfare

Masks. Some Eskimo masks were made from whalebone.

Paint Brushes. The Plains Indians made paint brushes from the soft matrix area of bone.

Scrapers. These were usually flat pieces of bone or antler with the edges sharpened for the removal of hair, fat, and other tissue from animal hides.

Whistles. Some of the Western tribes used bird bones to make whistles. Collectors will find very nicely made bird bone whistles available. Some are even etched.

Other items. The prehistoric and historic American Indians made jewelry, small needles, and spoons among other items. The method of manufacturing bone items was to carve and abrade the bone with stone tools.

Areas of origin consist of almost all areas where American Indians lived. American Indian bone tools, jewelry pieces, and weapons are not highly collected but are available and inexpensive.

Other bone artifacts are:

arrowheads	incisors (Northwest)
barbs	needles (drilled eyes)
bark beaters (Northwest)	needles (incised eyes)
bark shredders	net gauges (Northwest)
beads	pendants
blanket pins	rings
charms	small pestles
fish gorgets	spindle whorls
hair pieces	spoons
handles	tooth pendants
harpoon points (barbed)	wedges
incisors (beaver teeth)	

Horn artifacts

Many of the animals that the American Indians killed for food, including buffalo, deer, mountain goats, elk, and antelope, had horns. Why throw away a hard-surfaced product that could be made into tools, jewelry, and many other items? Prehistoric and historic tribes used the horns to make the following:

Jewelry items. Beads, fetishes, and pendants were made in prehistoric and into the early historic period.

Arrowheads. Some arrowheads were made from the sharp tips of horns.

Flinting tools. The fine pressure work on arrowheads and spears was done with a piece of deer horn. The percussion work was done with mallets made from dense elk horn.

Picks. Some picks for digging were made from horn.

Spoons. Beautiful spoons were made by the Northwest American Indians from the horns of the mountain goat. Boiling the horn made it more pliable for formation into spoons. The handles were carved into totem symbols and other figures. Some Northern California tribes as well as the Plains tribes also made spoons from horn.

Wedges. Horn wedges cut from elk or large horn animals were used by the Northwest tribes to split wood by driving horn wedges into wood.

SHELL ARTIFACTS

Sea and fresh water shells were used by the American Indian from prehistoric times until the present to make jewelry, tools, and ceremonial items.

Shell was worked by cutting, abrading, and smoothing. The Hohokam tribes of Arizona even developed a way to acid-etch shell by fermenting cactus juice.

The items made of shell in prehistoric times are the following:

Fish hooks. These were crafted by the California Chumash as well as other tribes.

Hoes. Small hoes for digging were sometimes made.

Jewelry. Fine small fetishes, bracelets, pendants, and necklaces of shell beads were beautifully made. Carved shell bracelets made in exquisite relief were produced by the Hohokam.

Spoons. American Indians of the Gulf area, Northwest, West, and East made use of shells as spoons. Some were adapted to the shapes of spoons, while others were used as is.

Other shell artifacts:

arrowheads	gorgets
rings	beads
nose rings	shell rattles
earrings	pendants

IVORY ARTIFACTS

This hard material from the walrus and the whale has been used for thousands of years to make tools, weapons, utility pieces, and jewelry by the many tribes of the Arctic and Subarctic areas. Ivory items are constructed by abrading, drilling, cutting, and smoothing. Fossilized ivory tools and dolls from these areas are very collectible.

Items made from ivory by the Northern tribes are:

blades	combs
harpoons	net gauges
bows	dolls
heddles	pipes
charms	fetishes
jewelry	snow goggles
clubs	hairpins
knives	tools

COLLECTING

Flint collectors often specialize in one of the following categories:

1. Pieces from one period of time such as Paleo
2. Pieces from one geographical region
3. Pieces of one type: all bird points, etc.
4. Pieces made of special stone material
5. Pieces of one usage: all knives, spears, etc.

Of course, many collections are made up of every type of stone. Stone collectors of picked, abraded, and polished artifacts will collect a mix of categories or specialize in:

1. One type: all bannerstones.
2. One material type: all slate, hard stone, etc.
3. One region: Midwest, etc.

A collector should choose the best method to identify a specific type of artifact. There are good books on flinted points, and I hope this book will assist you as well. To identify the types of stones, collect one small piece of each type and display them on a board. Being able to view the pieces side by side will assist you in identifying the material that each artifact in question is made of. Finer quality stones make more valuable pieces.

Arrowheads are grouped by their shapes. The steps in identifying a flinted point are:

1. Determine the shape.
2. Refer to the names of points given for that shape.
3. Check the pictures shown in *The Overstreet Indian and Identification Price Guide* for all the names of points with that shape until you find yours.
4. Match the size and quality to determine the approximate price.

One can acquire a collection of stone, bone, shell, horn, and ivory artifacts by field hunting, buying, and/or trading.

Field hunting is still very popular and a lot of fun, however some states are passing laws to stop field hunting. The Midwest still produces some good finds in stone.

Buying stone, bone, shell, horn, and ivory items is enjoyable until you purchase your first fake. Unfortunately, the area of American Indian stone collectibles is heavy with reproductions. This is due to the fact that there are expert flinters that can produce hard-to-detect reproductions. Usually it is not the creator of the new piece who is dishonest, but the later owners. However, one should not give up such a fun collectible as stone artifacts. By finding your own in the field and purchasing only from reputable dealers and collectors, you can build a very valuable authentic collection. To purchase, sell, or trade stone, bone, shell, horn, and ivory items there are shows, dealers' trade newspapers, American Indian stores, and auctions where you can get what you want.

QUALITY DETERMINATION

Quality of flint points is graded on a scale of 1 to 10, with 10 being best.

Authentic stone collectible quality is determined by:

1. craftsmanship
2. shape
3. quality of stone
4. condition

Bone, horn, shell, and ivory quality is determined by workmanship and condition.

DISPLAYING AND STORING

Arrowheads and other small artifacts are best displayed in glass frames. Today's frames hold the artifacts in place with no glue or wires needed, yet the front of the glass frame can be opened and items handled. Wall displays can be done by hanging the frames. There are a number of companies selling these frames very inexpensively. If you are going to pay hundreds of dollars for artifacts, spend a little on the cabinets and frames that display the artifact as well as protect it.

Larger stone, bone, shell, horn, and ivory pieces look good on open shelves or in larger glass cabinets. Large mortars and metates can be displayed around the fireplace, on the porch, or in the garden. If you have to store any of these items, do so in a manner that prevents breakage or chipping.

Water and/or a little soap will clean grime off most of these pieces. If you have sticky matter on any of these items, try alcohol or acetone to remove it. Too often, the identification stickers put on these items leave a stain and a sticky spot when removed.

REPAIRING

All pieces in this chapter can be repaired to make them look better, but a repaired piece is less desirable and valuable. As with any collectible, buy the best you can afford, and try to buy only unrepaired or unbroken pieces.

CATALOGING AND INSURANCE

Good record keeping of your more valuable stone, bone, shell, horn, and ivory items with a number assigned to each is recommended. Using typing whiteout to make a small area for a number to be applied works well.

It is your choice to insure or not to insure. Insurance has become so expensive that it is now practically prohibitive.

MARKET CONDITIONS

The collecting of prehistoric stone, bone, shell, horn, and invory is in transition but the market is still very strong. There are some collectors switching to other forms of American Indian collectibles, thereby putting more stone, bone, shell, horn, and ivory on the market. However, there is such good demand for quality pieces that the market has held firm. Sure, years ago the market was much lower, but there are more new collectors coming in and demand is high. What the future holds for us I cannot predict, but one thing is certain: high quality authentic stone, bone, shell, horn, and ivory artifacts are going to get more scarce.

APPRAISALS

If you are going to insure your collection, an appraisal is needed. If you are going to sell or trade and do not know your values, you will need an appraisal. Always use an appraiser who is in the market every day, either trading or selling. Too often appraisers are hired who do not know the item they are appraising.

9

GENERAL INFORMATION

To assist you, the collector, in further studies on American Indian art and artifacts, listed below are sources of information on the following: museums and state parks; periodicals; videos; shows and promoters; and reading material.

MUSEUMS AND STATE PARKS

Alaska State Museum, Juneau, Alaska

American Museum of Natural History, New York, New York

Amerind Foundation, Inc., Dragoon, Alaska

Anchorage Historical and Fine Arts Museum, Anchorage, Alaska

Arizona Museum, Tucson, Arizona

Brooklyn Museum, Brooklyn, New York

Buffalo Bill Historical Center, Cody, Wyoming

Cahokia Mounds, Collinsville, Illinois

Colorado History Museum, Denver, Colorado

Crazy Horse Memorial, Crazy Horse, South Dakota

Denver Museum of Natural History, Denver, Colorado

Des Moines Art Center, Des Moines, Iowa

Etowah Mounds State Historical Site, Cartersville, Georgia

Favell Museum, Klamath Falls, Oregon

Field Museum of Natural History, Chicago, Illinois

Florida Museum of Natural History, Gainsville, Florida

Fruitlands American Indian Museum, Harvard, Massachusetts

Gateway Arch Museum, St. Louis, Missouri

Gilscrease Museum, Tulsa, Oklahoma

Haffenreffer Museum of Anthropology, Bristol, Rhode Island

The Heard Museum, Phoenix, Arizona

High Desert Museum, Bend, Oregon

Howe Art Museum, Coral Gables, Florida

Hudson Museum, Orono, Maine

Iroquois Indian Museum, Howes Cave, New York

Joslyn Art Museum, Omaha, Nebraska

Kolomoki Mounds State Museum, Blakely, Georgia

Lowie Museum of Anthropology, Berkeley, California

Makah Museum, Neah Bay, Washington

Malki Museum, Morongo Indian Reservation, Banning, California

Maryhill Museum of Art, Goldendale, Washington

Maxwell Museum of Anthropology, Albuquerque, New Mexico

Mid-American All Indian Center, Wichita, Kansas

Mille Lacs Indian Museum, Onomia, Minnesota

Millicent Rogers Museum, Taos, New Mexico

Minnesota Historical Society, St. Paul, Minnesota

Mitchell Indian Museum, Evanston, Illinois

Montclair Art Museum, Montclair, New Jersey

Mt. Kearsarge Indian Museum, Warner, New Hampshire

Museum of Anthropology, Winston-Salem, North Carolina

Museum of Indian Arts and Culture, Santa Fe, New Mexico

Museum of Northern Arizona, Flagstaff, Arizona

Museum of the Plains Indians, Browning, Montana

Museum of the Rockies, Boseman, Montana

Museum of Warm Springs, Warm Springs, Oregon

National Museum of the American Indian, New York, New York

National Museum of Natural History, Washington, D.C.

Natural History Museum of Los Angeles County, Los Angeles,
   California

North Dakota Museum of Art, Grand Forks, North Dakota

Oakland Museum, Oakland, California

Osage Indian Museum, Pawkuska, Oklahoma

Owens Valley Paiute Shoshone Cultural Center, Bishop, California

Palm Springs Museum, Palm Springs, California

Panhandle-Plains Historical Museum, Canyon, Texas

Plains Indian Museum, Cody, Wyoming

Plenty Coups State Park, Pryor, Montana

Pueblo Grande Museum, Phoenix, Arizona

Reese Bullen Gallery, Arcata, California

San Diego Museum of Man, San Diego, California

Santa Barbara Museum of Natural History, Santa Barbara, California

Seattle Art Museum, Seattle, Washington

Sherman Indian Museum, Riverside, California

Sioux Indian Museum, Rapid City, South Dakota

Southwest Museum, Los Angeles, California

Turtle Mountain Indian Historical Society, Belcourt, North Dakota

University of Colorado, Boulder, Colorado

University Museum of Archaeology and Anthropology, Philadelphia,
   Pennsylvania

University of Nebraska State Museum, Lincoln, Nebraska

White Mountain Archaeological Center and Raven Site Ruin,
    St. Johns, Arizona

As previously mentioned, when planning a visit to any museum, be sure
to check the visiting hours. Also, if traveling, be sure to check the local
phone book or contact the Chamber of Commerce for the names of
museums, as there are many small ones with great collections, and these
should not be overlooked.

The periodicals listed below are only a few that are published nationwide.
There are many that are published locally, so check your local phone book
or the phone book in the areas where you may be traveling for more listings.
You may also contact any of the periodicals listed here for more information.

American Indian Art
7314 E. Osborn
Scottsdale, AZ 85251

Native Peoples
P.O. Box 36830
Phoenix, AZ 85026

Cowboys and Indians
1800 Wyatt Drive
Suite 10
Santa Clara, CA 95054

Prehistoric Antiquities
P.O. Box 296
North Lewisburg, OH 43060

The Indian Trader
P.O. Box 1421
Gallup, NM 87301

I am going to name only a few videos that I think you would be interested
in viewing. These videos are very educational yet fun. Please contact the
producer of each video for more information regarding availablility, cost, etc.
There are many more videos that I could mention, but these are a few of the
best, in my opinion.

A Treasury of California Baskets and Baskets of the the Northwest People
Mimbres Fever
2403 Earl St.
Los Angeles, CA 90039
213-669-0761

The Art of Navajo Weaving, The Durango Collection
Interpark
1540 E. MacArthur
Cortez, CO 91321
303-565-7453

The California Indian Art Association has over 20 videos that are not professionally produced but offer lots of information on Southern California American Indians.

California Indian Arts Association
c/o Justin Farmer
1954 Evergreen Ave.
Fullerton, CA 92635
714-256-1269

This next group of videos are the products of worldwide university students. The price to purchase these videos covers only the cost to reproduce including the time, the tapes, and any other expenses incurred during reproduction.

The Human Journey: Stone Implements
The Human Journey: Cog Stones
The Human Journey: Various interviews with prominent people
  within the American Indian community

Ellen Woods
P.O. Box 60
Salinas, CA 93902-0060
408-449-1136

The following is a list of shows and their promotors:

American Indian Antiques
Roy Harrell
P.O. Box 5
Kingsville, MD 21087

American Indian Show
400 W. Alondra Blvd.
Gardena, CA 90248

American Indian and
 Traders Guild
Laurie Richardson
3876 E. Fadora Ave.
Fresno, CA 93726

American Indian and Western
 Relic Show
8900 N. Vancouver Ave.
Portland, OR 97217

Don Bennett's
Whitehawk's Inc.
P.O. Box 283
Agoura, CA 91376

Gateway Indian Art Club
Elaine Tucker
7755 Mohawk
St. Louis, MO 63105

High Noon
9929 Venice Blvd.
Los Angeles, CA 90034

MCM Productions
Kim Martindale
38 W. Main St.
Ventura, CA 93001

Renaissance Promotions
Eric and Jeannie Nordell
15746 Bradner Rd.
Northville, MI 48167

Roving Galleries
Harry and Toots LaFavor
221 Reservation Dr.
Parker, AZ 85344

There are many other shows taking place throughout the United States. Please check the periodicals and contact the producers of the shows above as both will be able to give you more information. Of the shows mentioned, some are strictly for antique Indian items only, while others carry both antique and contemporary.

Mortars and pestles, California. Left, Chumash; right, Yosemite Valley.

GLOSSARY

Abrade. To smooth over a rough surface.

Aniline dye. A synthetic dye.

Annealing. The tempering of metal by heating and rapid cooling.

Appliqué. The method of decoration where added pieces of clay are applied on a wet pot to build up the design.

Atlatl. A device with an arm used to leverage force onto a small spear.

Awl. A tool used by the weavers to pierce holes on the surface of the basket for the weft material to pass through.

Baleen. The black fibrous material from a whale's mouth shredded for weaving.

Bandolier. A beaded shoulder bag with a wide beaded strap that goes around the shoulder and/or neck.

Bannerstone. A polished stone used as a weight.

Basal corner. The corner on the back end of a spear point.

Batten. A thin, flat wooden stick.

Bayeta. A commercial wool fabric, usually red, that the Southwest weavers unravelled and used in their early weaving.

BCE. Before Common Era.

Bear grass. A plant that grows in Northern California and Oregon and gives an off-white color to baskets.

Bezel. A strip of silver around a stone to hold it to the backing.

Bifaced. Two-sided.

Bird quill. The stems from bird feathers dyed and used by American Indians for decoration.

Bit. The sharp bladed area on an axe.

Bola. A neck slide usually decorated.

Border. A band woven around a rug to set it off like a frame.

Bottleneck. A squat-shaped basket with a shoulder finishing in a narrow neck.

Bracken fern. The pithy, black material collected from the root of the fern. This provided the black color in the baskets.

Brain tanned. The American Indian process of curing leather by using animal brains and a liquid.

Burden. An American Indian utilitarian basket used to carry objects, usually cone-shaped but can have a rounded bottom.

Cannel coal. A bituminous coal containing much volatile matter that burns brightly.

Carding paddle. A tooth-surfaced board used to untangle wool fibers.

Casting. The formation of items by pouring liquid hot metals into a mold and cooling it to a hard form.

Catlinite. The soft red stone used in the making of pipes.

CE. Common Era.

Chasing. The chisel and hammer decoration on metal.

Chief's blanket. A striped wearing blanket woven wider than long. Used by Plains Indian chiefs; there are three phases of this blanket.

Child's serape. Small weaving blanket about 30" x 48" that is a small version of the Navajo serape.

Clapper. A noise maker to scare away evil spirits, used by the Northwest tribes.

Classic Period. The time period from 1850 to 1868 in Southwest weaving.

Cochineal dye. A red powder from ground-up insect carcasses of the New World.

Coiling (baskets). A method of construction where grass, rods, or combination of both are worked in a circular fashion with a weft woven around the coil.

Coiling (pottery). The method of pottery construction where rolled out, thin coils of clay are stacked on top of each other to form the walls of the pot.

Commercial yarn. Machine-made woolen yarn.

Corrugated. Pottery coils, when wet, are indented on the outside to give a rough texture that looks parallel-grooved and ridged.

Cordage. A hemplike material or native grass.

Crescent. A quarter moon-shaped object.

Cross-hatching. The design work where fine parallel lines are used to fill space.

Crupper. Functional horse regalia with a strap that goes under a horse's tail to keep its saddle from sliding forward.

Curvilinear. A line that has no straight parts.

Cut-out. A form of decorating where pieces of hide or cloth are removed to create a design.

Dentalium. The long cone-shaped sea shell from the Northwest Coast.

Devil's claw. A seed pod with a long neck and two very sharp hooks. The pods are peeled back to get to the black fibers in the hooks; this produces the black in most Southwest and some California baskets.

Drawshave. A tool consisting of a blade with a handle at each end for use in shaving off surfaces; a drawknife.

Embossing. To decorate with raised designs above the surface.

Eye Dazzler. A style of Navajo weaving done with striking serrated zigzag lines in very bright colors.

Fag. The slanting end of the sewing stitch.

Ferruginous. Containing iron, as in a stone.

Fired. The process whereby pottery is baked at a high temperature to make it very hard.

Fletching. The application of feathers to the back end of an arrow.

Flinter. One who makes arrowheads and spear points from stone using percussion and/or pressure to remove and shape the stone.

Foundation. In the manufacturing of a basket this includes the coils, splints, or warps used to give the basket its main structural support.

Gauntlets. A pair of gloves.

Gemstone. A high quality stone, usually agate, jasper, jade, quartz, petrified wood, or chalcedony.

Germantown. A yarn of very bright colors produced in the United States commercially of 3- or 4-ply synthetic dyes, used by the Navajo in 1870.

Gilt-faceted beads. Beads with cut edges used from 1865 to 1895.

Glazed. The painted material on pottery that melts during firing causing a glassy surface while resolidifying.

Gorget. A bone, shell, or stone which is perforated so that it can be suspended.

Hafting. The application of a handle to a stone or metal piece.

Handspun yarn. Yarn made from handspinning raw wool.

Hatched. To mark or engrave with fine, crossed, or parallel lines to indicate shading.

Heddle. Wood sticks used to control the warps of the weaving.

Hematin. A compound containing iron.

Historic. The period of time after the arrival of the Europeans, until the mid–1900s.

Imbrication. A decoration or pattern created by an overlapping of edges.

Imprint. The marking in wet clay with a formed object to make a design inward on the surface.

Incised. A method of decoration in which patterns are scratched on clay before the pot is fired.

Incurvate. To curve inward.

Indigo. Blue-colored plant dye brought to the Southwest by the Spanish and used by the Navajo for the blue color in their early weavings.

Jade. A hard green glossy stone (nephrite).

Jar. A vessel taller than a bowl that has an opening narrower than its greatest width.

Jet. A lightweight black stone (lignite).

Joshua tree root. The Joshua tree grows in the deserts of Southeastern California and a small section of Arizona. This plant produces the color red in baskets from those areas.

Juncas. A plant that grows in Southern California and gives the coloring of a golden amber to a mottled color.

Ketoh. A bow guard for protection of the wrist.

Kiva bowls. Bowls used in the kiva, an underground chamber for ceremonial purposes.

Labret. A piece used to fill and decorate the lip or ear-pierced hole.

Lanceolate. A narrow and tapered leaf-shaped arrowhead or spearhead.

Late Classic Period. 1865 to 1875 in Southwest weaving.

Loom. A frame for weaving thread or yarn into cloth.

Manta. A woman's shawl wider than it is long.

Martingale. Part of the harness of a horse that hangs from the neck and covers the breast, usually decorated with beads.

Martynia. A weed that grows in California and Arizona and has a hooked seed pod (a devil's claw).

Matrix. The center of bone where the tissue matter is soft.

Matte. A metallic-like dark finish on pottery caused by a vegetable or mineral paint that does not melt during firing.

Micaceous. Clay that has mica flakes in it.

Midden. A pile of refuse from shore-dwelling prehistoric people.

Mineral. Neither animal or vegetable, a mineral is inorganic, used for painting of pottery.

Moki weaving. A weaving with a blue banded background into which brown and white stripes are incorporated, and with light red terraced and serrated designs.

Monolithic. A single piece of stone.

Mordant. A chemical that fixes a dye by combining with it to form a compound.

Mosaic inlay. Decoration done with small tiles of stone glued closely together to form designs.

Motif. A scheme of designs created in a pattern.

Naja. A crescent-shaped ornament formally used as a forehead pendant on horse gear. Later used as a necklace pendant.

Node. A knoblike clay attachment added to the pottery surface for decoration.

Notch. The groove made on a point where attachment was made to the shaft of an arrow or spear.

Olla. A globular pottery vessel with a small opening and usually a short neck.

Organic. A plant substance used in the painting of pottery.

Overlay. The method used by the Hopi to make designs with metal where a silver sheet with cutouts is laid over another sheet of metal.

Paleo. Describes an ancient age before the modern era when stone tools and weapons were made by Early Man.

Patina. A surface appearance of something grown beautiful with age or use.

Pawn. American Indian items made and worn, then used to borrow money or to pay for other items at the trading posts.

Pecking. The method of making stone items where harder stone is struck against a softer stone to remove the pieces.

Plaiting. The method of weaving where the warp and the wefts are the same size and woven at right angles to each other.

Plaque. A dish or tray-shaped basket.

Poll. The butt end of an axe.

Polychrome. More than two colors.

Popeye. An effigy form where both eyes protrude out of the side of the head.

Porphyry. A very hard rock having a dark, purplish red groundmass containing small crystals of feldspar.

Prehistoric. The period before there were written records; before the coming of the Europeans to America.

Pre-reservation period. The period before the American Indians were moved to reservations. The accepted date for this period is before 1880.

Possible bag. A beaded or quilled bag large enough to carry the owner's belongings.

Punctate. A method of design where piercing marks are made on the wet pottery surface.

Quirt. Riding whip.

Quiver. A case for a bow and arrows.

Reamer. A rotating tool with cutting edges used to enlarge or shape a hole.

Regional rug. Made in one of the 13 weaving areas of the Navajo.

Repoussé. This is relief design work on a flat surface where the pattern is raised from the reverse side.

Rods. The even-sized sticks used to form the coils.

Redbud. A bush which produces the red coloring in the baskets of Northern California.

Regional rug. Made in one of the 13 weaving areas of the Navajo.

Reservation period. The period from 1880–1920 when American Indians were restricted to reservations.

Saddle blanket. A blanket woven to be used under a horse's saddle.

Sandpainting weaving. A weaving depicting one of the Navajo sandpainting ceremonies.

Saxony. A fine 3-ply yarn with silky texture, commercially made in Europe, dyed with presynthetic natural dye.

Sedge. The root from grass, spliced for the sewing weft of many baskets. The coloring it provides is a blondish golden tone.

Serape. A finely woven blanket longer than wide made in the 1800s with natural wools, bayeta, saxony, and indigo only.

Serrated. A saw-like edge.

Sinew. Thread made from the tendons of animals.

Slip. A mixture of fine clay put on the outside of a pottery piece to make a better surface for painting.

Sotol. A plant related to the agave family that resembles a yucca.

Spidery appendage. A descriptive term for the designs used mainly by the Sioux after 1875. The design spreads out with appendages like the legs of a spider.

Spirit break. The unpainted section (approx. 1/2 in.) of a painted rim.

Stamping. Making designs on metal with a tool that has the pattern carved into it, or with a hammer.

Start. The beginning coils of the basket.

Stem. The protruding back part of an arrowhead or spear.

Studded. The decoration of hide objects with tacks or studs.

Tab. A small pendant usually rectangular and drilled.

Temper. An inert material mixed with clay to reduce the cracking during drying and firing.

Totemic figures. Stylized animals, humans, and creatures of the Northwest tribes.

Transitional Period. 1868 to 1890 in Southwest weaving. The period when the weavers changed from blankets to rugs.

Tufa. A soft stone easily carved, used to make molds in casting.

Twining. The method used to weave baskets where two or more flexible weft strands are woven between vertical warps.

Vegetal dye. Dye from a plant source.

Wampum. White and purple shell beads used by the early Eastern American Indians to make belts, necklaces, and many other items.

Warp. In weaving, the vertical strand of material.

Weft. In weaving, the horizontal strand of material.

Whimsies. Tourist items of beadwork made by the American Indians near Niagara Falls from the 1890s to around 1915.

Winnowing tray. An open woven basket used to separate seed from the shaft.

Yei. Spiritual being.

Yeii'bicheii. Design figures of supernatural beings that are shown on rugs either dancing or in profile.

Yucca Root. The yucca plant is found throughout the deserts of California, Arizona, and Nevada, giving the color of red to baskets from these areas.

BIBLIOGRAPHY

Chapter 2. American Indian Baskets

Allen, Elsie. 1972. *Pomo Basket Making: A Supreme Art for the Weaver.* Happy Camp, CA: Naturegraph Publishers, Inc.

Bates, Craig D., and Martha J. Lee. 1990. *Tradition and Innovation: A Basket History of the Yosemite-Mono Lake Area.* Yosemite National Park: Yosemite Association.

James, George Wharton. 1903. *Indian Basketry, and How to Make Indian and Other Baskets.* Pasadena, CA: George Wharton James.

Kissell, Mary Lois. 1974. *Basketry of the Papago and Pima Indians.* Glorieta, NM: The Rio Grande Press, Inc.

Lamb, Frank W. 1981. *Indian Baskets of North America.* La Pine, OR: Rubidoux Publishing Co.

Linn, Natalie. 1993. *The Plateau Bag: A Tradition in Native American Weaving.* Johnson County Community College, Gallery of Art.

Lobb, Allan. *Indian Baskets of the Pacific Northwest and Alaska.* Portland, OR: Graphic Arts Center Publishing Co.

Lopez, Raul A., and Christopher L. Moser. 1981. *Rods, Bundles, and Stitches: A Century of Southern California Indian Basketry.* Riverside, CA: Riverside Museum Press.

Miles, Thomas E. 1983. *The Pueblo Children of the Earth Mother,* I & II. New York: Doubleday and Co.

Mason, Otis Tufton. 1976. *Aboriginal American Indian Basketry: Studies in a Textile Art Without Machinery.*

Moser, Christopher L.
1986. *Native American Basketry of Central California.*
1989. *Native American Indian Basketry of Northern California.*
1993. *Native American Basketry of Southern California.*
Riverside, CA: Riverside Museum Press.

Paul, Frances. 1944. *Spruce Root Basketry of the Alaska Tlingit.* Dept. of the Interior: Haskell Institute.

Roberts, Helen H. 1974. *Basketry of the San Carlos Apache Indians.* Glorieta, NM: The Rio Grande Press, Inc.

Silva, Arthur M., and William C. Cane. 1976. *California Indian Basketry: An Artistic Overview.* Cypress, CA: College Fine Arts Gallery.

Turnbaugh, Sarah Peabody, and William A. Turnbaugh. 1986. *Indian Baskets.* West Chester, PA: Schiffer Publishing, Ltd.

Whiteford, Andrew Hunter. 1988. *Southwestern Indian Baskets; Their History and Their Makers.* Santa Fe, NM: School of American Research Press.

Chapter 3. American Indian Pottery

Batkin, Jonathan. 1987. *Pottery of the Pueblos of New Mexico, 1700–1940.* Colorado Springs: Colorado Springs Fine Arts Center.

Brody, J.J. 1977. *Mimbres Painted Pottery.* Albuquerque: University of New Mexico.

Brody, J.J., Catherine J. Scott, and Steven La Blanc. 1983. *Mimbres Pottery: Ancient Art of the American Southwest.* New York: Hudson Hills Press.

Breternitz, David A., Arthur H. Rohn, and Elizabeth Morris. 1974. *Prehistoric Ceramics of the Mesa Verde Region.* The Northern Arizona Society of Science and Art, Inc.

Crotty, Helen K. 1983. *Honoring the Dead, Anasazi Ceramics from the Rainbow Bridge-Monument Valley Expedition*. Los Angeles: UCLA Museum of Cultural History.

Dedera, Don. 1985. *Artistry in Clay*. Flagstaff, AZ: Northland Press.

Dillingham, Rick, with Melinda Elliott. 1992. *Acoma and Laguna Pottery*. Santa Fe, NM: School of American Research Press.

Dittert, Alfred E., Jr. 1980. *Generations in Clay: Pueblo Pottery of the American Southwest*. Flagstaff, AZ: Northland Press.

Fewkes, Jesse
1911. *Antiquities of the Mesa Verde National Park Cliff Palace*.
Washington Government Printing Office.
1973. *Prehistoric Hopi Pottery Designs*. New York: Doreer Publications Inc.

Frank, Larry, and Francis H. Harlow. 1974. *Historic Pottery of the Pueblo Indians 1600–1880*. Boston: New York Graphic Society, Ltd.

Gill, Spencer (text), and Jerry Jacka (photography). 1976. *Pottery Treasures, The Splendor of Southwest Indian Art*. Portland, OR: Graphic Arts Center Publishing Company.

Gladwin, Harold S., et al. 1965. *Excavations at Snaketown*. Tucson: University of Arizona Press.

Hardin, Margaret Ann. 1983. *Gifts of Mother Earth: Ceramics in the Zuni Tradition*. Phoenix: The Heard Museum.

Harlow, Francis, H. 1990. *Two Hundred Years of Historic Pueblo Pottery: The Gallegos Collection*. Santa Fe, NM: Morning Star Gallery.

Hathcock, Roy
1983. *The Quapaw and Their Pottery*. Camden, AK: Hurley Press, Inc.
1988. *Ancient Indian Pottery of the Mississippi River Valley*. Marceline, MO: Walsworth Publishing Co.

Lister, Robert H., and Florence C. Lister. 1978. *Anasazi Pottery*. Albuquerque: University of New Mexico Press.

Madsen, Rex. E. 1977. *Prehistoric Ceramics of the Fremont*. Flagstaff, AZ: Museum of Northern Arizona.

Martin, Paul S., and Elizabeth S. Willis. 1977. *Anasazi Painted Pottery in Field Museum of Natural History*. Millwood, NY: Kraus Reprint Co.

Mouland, Barbara L. 1981. *Within the Underworld Sky, Mimbres Ceramic Art in Context*. Japan: Twelve Tree Press.

Noble, David Grant, ed. 1991. *The Hohokam: Ancient People of the Desert*. Santa Fe, NM: School of American Research Press.

Peckham, Stewart. 1990. *From This Earth, The Ancient Art of Pueblo Pottery*. Santa Fe, NM: Museum of New Mexico Press.

Rodee, Marian, and James Ostler. 1986. *Zuni Pottery*. West Chester, PA: Schiffer Publishing, Ltd.

Spivey, Richard L. 1979. *Maria*. Flagstaff, AZ: Northland Press.

Toulouse, Betty. 1977. *Pueblo Pottery of the New Mexico Indians*. Santa Fe, NM: Museum of New Mexico Press.

Turner, Barry, and Elaine Turner. 1990. *Ceramic Art of the Prehistoric Southwest*. Oklahoma City: Able Concepts.

Chapter 4. Quillwork, Beadwork, and Other American Indian Collectibles

Bebbiangton, Julia, M. *Quillwork of the Plains*. Canada: Glenbow Museum.

Brafford, C.J., and Thom Laine. 1992. *Dancing Colors: Paths of Native American Women*. San Francisco: Chronicle Books.

Brasser, Ted J. 1976. *"Bo'jou, Neejee!" Profiles of Canadian Indian Art*. Canada: Apex Press Limited.

Conn, Richard
   1979. *Native American Art*.
   1982. *Circles of the World*.
   1986. *A Persistent Vision: Art of the Reservation Days*.
   Denver Art Museum.

Dublin, Lois Sherr. *The History of Beads: From 30,000 BC to Present*. New York: Harry N. Abrams Publishers, Inc.

Duncan, Kate C. 1989. *Northern Athapaskan Art: A Beadwork Tradition*. Seattle: University of Washington Press.

Ewers, John C. 1945. *Blackfeet Crafts*. Lawrence, KS: Haskell Institute.

Ferg, Alan. 1987. *Western Apache Material Culture: The Goodwin and Guenther Collections*. Tucson: University of Arizona Press.

Hail, Barbara, A. 1980. *Hau, Kola!: The Plains Indian Collection of the Haffenreffer Museum of Anthropology*, Bristol, RI: Eastern Press, Inc.

Hedges, Ken, ed. 1995. *And the Bead Goes On! The Vision Persists: Native Folk Arts of the West*. San Diego: Museum of Man.

Herbst, Toby, and Joel Kopp. 1993. *The Flag in American Indian Art*. Seattle: University of Washington Press.

Horse Capture, George P., and Richard A. Phort. 1986. *Salish Indian Art: From the J.R. Simplot Collection*. Moscow, ID: North Country Book Express, Inc.

Kopper, Philip. 1986. *The Smithsonian Book of North American Indians Before the Coming of the Europeans*. Washington, DC: Smithsonian Books.

Lenz, Mary Jane. 1986. *The Stuff of Dreams: Native American Dolls*. New York: National Museum of the American Indian.

Lyford, Carrie
   1940. *Quill and Beadwork of the Western Sioux*. Lawrence, KS: Haskell Institute.
   1953. *Ojibwa Crafts (Chippewa)*. Phoenix: Indian School Print Shop.

Mails, Thomas E.
   1972. *Mystic Warriors of the Plains*. New York: Mallard Press.
   1973. *Plains Indians: Dog Soldiers, Bear Men and Buffalo Women*.
   New York: Bonanza Books.
   1974. *A People Called Apache*. New York: BDD Illustrated Books.

Markoe, Glen E. 1986. *Vestiges of a Proud Nation: The Odgen B. Read Northern Plains Indian Collection*. Lincoln, NE: University of Nebraska Press.

Maurer, Evan M. 1992. *Visions of the People: A Pictorial History of Plains Indian Life*. Minneapolis: The Minneapolis Institute of Arts.

O'Connor, Nancy Fields. 1984. *Fred E. Miller: Photographer of the Crows*. University of Montana.

Pettit, Jan. 1990. *Utes, the Mountain People*. Boulder, CO: Johnson Publishing Company.

Scriver, Bob. 1990. *The Blackfeet Artists of the Northern Plains: The Scriver Collection of Blackfeet Indian Artifacts and Related Objects, 1894–1990*. Kansas City, KS: The Lowell Press, Inc.

Thom, Laine. 1992. *Becoming Brave: The Path to Native American Manhood*. San Francisco: Chronicle Books.

Torrence, Gaylord, and Robert Hobbs. 1989. *The Mesquakie of Iowa: Art of the Red Earth People*. Seattle: University of Washington Press.

Walton, Anne T., John C. Evers., and Royal B. Hassrick. 1985. *After the Buffalo Were Gone: The Louis Warren Hill Sr. Collection of Indian Art*. St. Paul, MN: Northeast Area Foundation.

Whitehead, Ruth Holmes. 1982. *Micmac Quillwork: Micmac Indian Techniques of Porcupine Quill Decoration: 1600–1959*. Halifax, Nova Scotia: The Nova Scotia Museum of Canada.

Chapter 5. Wood and Hide Collectibles

Burnham, Dorothy K. 1992. *To Please the Caribou*. Seattle: University of Washington Press.

Collins, Henry B., et al. 1977. *The Far North, 2000 Years of American Eskimo and Indian Art*. Bloomington, ID: Indiana University Press.

Fenton, William N. 1987. *The False Faces of the Iroquois*. Norman, OK: University of Oklahoma Press.

Fewkes, Jesse Walter. 1962. *Hopi Kachinas Drawn by Native Artists*. Chicago: The Rio Grande Press Inc.

Fitzhugh, William W., and Aron Crowell. 1988. *Crossroads of Continents, Cultures of Siberia and Alaska*. Seattle: Smithsonian Institution Press.

Garfield, Viola E., and Linn A. Forrest. 1948. *The Wolf and the Raven*. Seattle: University of Washington Press.

Hawthorn, Audrey. 1988. *Kwakiutl Art*. Seattle: University of Washington Press.

Holm, Bill
1972. *Crooked Beak of Heaven*.
1987. *Spirit and Ancestor, A Century of Northwest Coast Indian Art at the Burke Museum*. Seattle: University of Washington Press.

Jonaitis, Aldona, ed. *Chiefly Feasts: The Enduring Kwakiutl Potlatch*. Seattle: University of Washington Press.

King, J.C.H. 1979. *Portrait Masks from the Northwest Coast of America*. London: Thames and Hudson.

Mason, Otis Tufton. 1972. *North American Bows, Arrows, and Quivers*. Carl J. Pugliese, Yonkers, NY.

Penny, David W. 1989. *Great Lakes Indian Art*. Detroit: Wayne State University Press and the Detroit Institute of Arts.

Torrence, Gaylord. 1994. *The American Indian Parfleche: A Tradition of Abstract Painting*. Seattle: University of Washington Press.

Wherry, Joseph H. 1969. *Indian Masks and Myths of the West*. New York: Funk and Wagnall.

Wright, Barton. 1973. *Kachinas, A Hopi Artist's Documentary*. Flagstaff & Phoenix: Northland Press with The Heard Museum.

Chapter 6. American Indian Weavings

Amsden, Charles Avery. 1934. *Navajo Weavings, Its Technique and History*. Santa Ana, CA: The Fine Arts Press.

Baer, Joshua. 1986. *Collecting the Navajo Child's Blanket*. Santa Fe, NM: Morning Star Gallery.

Blomberg, Nancy J. 1988. *Navajo Textiles: The William Randolph Hearst Collection*. Tucson: University of Arizona Press.

Campbell, Tyrone, and Joel and Kate Kopp. 1991. *Navajo Pictorial Weavings 1880–1950: Folk Art Images of Native Americans*. New York: Penguin Books USA.

James, George Wharton. 1974. *Indian Blankets and Their Makers*. New York: Dover Publications, Inc.

James, H.L. 1976. *Posts and Rugs, The Story of Navajo Rugs and Their Homes*. Globe, AZ: Southwest Parks and Monuments Assoc.

Kaufman, Alice, and Christopher Selser. 1985. *The Navajo Weaving Tradition 1650 to Present*.

Kent, Kate Peck. 1987. *Pueblo Indian Textiles, A Living Tradition*. Santa Fe, NM: School of American Research Press.

McIntyre, Kellen Kee. 1992. *Rio Grande Blankets: Late Nineteenth-Century Textiles in Transition*. Albuquerque: The Adobe Gallery.

Mera, H.P. 1987. *Spanish-American Blanketry*. Santa Fe, NM: School of American Research Press.

Rodee, Marian. 1987. *Weavings of the Southwest*. West Chester, PA: Schiffer Publishing, Ltd.

Chapter 7. American Indian Jewelry

Bahti, Mark. 1980. *Collecting Southwest Native American Jewelry*. New York: David McKay Company, Inc.

Bedinger, Margery. 1973. *Indian Silver: Navajo and Pueblo Jewelers*. Albuquerque: University of New Mexico Press.

Frank, Larry. 1990. *Indian Silver Jewelry of the Southwest 1868–1930*. West Chester, PA: Schiffer Publishing, Ltd.

Gill, Spencer. 1975. *Turquoise Treasures: The Splendor of Southwest Indian Art*. Portland, OR: Graphic Arts Center Publishing Company.

Jernigan, Westley E. *Jewelry of the Prehistoric Southwest*. Tucson: Dale Stuart King.

Jacka, Jerry D., and Nancy S. Hammack. 1975. *Indian Jewelry of the Prehistoric Southwest*. Tucson: University of Arizona Press.

Lincoln, Louise, ed. 1982. *Southwest Indian Silver from the Doneghy Collection*. Austin, TX: University of Texas Press.

Woodward, Arthur. 1971. *Navajo Silver*. Flagstaff, AZ: Northland Press.

Chapter 8. Stone, Bone, Horn, Shell, and Ivory Collectibles

Barnett, Franklin. 1973. *Dictionary of Prehistoric Indian Artifacts of the American Southwest*. Flagstaff, AZ: Northland Press.

Braidwood, Robert J. 1967. *Prehistoric Man*. Chicago: Scott, Foresman and Co.

Bierer, Bert N. 1980. *Indians and Artifacts in the Southwest*. Columbia, SC: The State Printing Co.

Converse, Robert N.
1973. *Ohio Flint Types, revised*.
1978. *Ohio Slate Types*. The Archaeological Society of Ohio.

Ewers, John C. 1979. *Indian Art in Pipestone: George Catlin's Portfolio in the British Museum*. Washington DC: British Museum Publications, Ltd, Smithsonian Institution Press.

Fundaburk, Emma Lila, and Mary Douglas Fundaburk Forman. 1957. *Sun Circles and Human Hands: The Southeastern Indians Art and Industries*. Luverne, AL: Emma Lila Fundaburk.

Furst, Peter J., and Jill L. Furst. 1982. *North American Art*. New York: Rizzoli International Publications, Inc.

Hothem, Lar
1983. *Arrowheads and Projectile Points Identification and Values*.
1991. *Indian Axes and Related Stone Artifacts*.
1992. *Indian Artifacts of the Midwest*.
1995. *Indian Artifacts of the Midwest #2*.
Paducah, KY: Collector Books.
1986. *Collecting Indian Knives: Identification and Values*.
1994. *Ancient Art of Ohio*.
1994. *North American Indian Artifacts*, 5th Edition.
Lancaster, OH: Hothem House Books.

Howe, Carrol B.
1972. *Ancient Tribes of Klamath Country*.
1979. *Ancient Modocs of California and Oregon*.
Portland, OR: Binford and Mort.

Knoblock, Bryan W. 1939. *Bannerstones of the North American Indian*. La Grange, IL: Bryon W. Knoblock.

Miles, Charles. 1963. *Indian and Eskimo Artifacts of North America*. Chicago: Henry Regnery Company.

Miller, Bruce, W. 1988. *Chumash: A Picture of Their World*. Los Osos, CA: Sand River Press.

Moorehead, Warren K. 1900. *Prehistoric Implements: Wilson Co., Tennessee*. Union City, GA: Charles G. Drake.

Overstreet, Robert M., and Howard Peake
1989. *The Overstreet Indian Projectile Points: Identification and Price Guide*, 1st ed. Cleveland, TN: Overstreet Publications Inc.
1991. *The Overstreet Indian Arrowheads: Identification and Price Guide*, 2d ed. New York: The House of Collectibles.
1993. *The Overstreet Indian Arrowheads Identification Guide*, 3d ed.
1995. *The Overstreet Indian Arrowheads Identification Guide*, 4th ed.
New York: Avon Books.

Perino, Gregory. 1985. *Selected Preforms, Points, and Knives of the North American Indians*. Idabel, OK: Gregory Perino.

Seaman, N.G. 1974. *Indian Relics of the Pacific Northwest*. Portland, OR: Binford and Mort.

Steward, Hilary. 1973. *Artifacts of the Northwest Coast Indian*. Saanichton, BC, Canada: Hancock House Publishers.

Strong, Emory
1976. *Stone Age in the Great Basin*.
1982. *Stone Age on the Columbia River*.
Portland, OR: Binford and Mort.

Thiry, Paul and Mary. 1977. *Eskimo Artifacts: Designed for Use*. Seattle: Superior Publishing Co.

Tully, Lawrence N. 1986. *Flint Blades and Projectile Points of the North American Indian*. Paducah, KY: Collector Books.

Waldorf, D.C., and Valerie Waldorf. 1979. *Flint Types of the Continental United States*. D.C. Waldorf.

Wedel, Waldo R. 1961, *Prehistoric Man on the Great Plains*. Norman, OK: University of Oklahoma Press.

Wormington, H.M. 1964. *Ancient Man of North America*. Denver: Museum of Natural History.

If you would like to order additional copies of *American Indian Artifacts* please complete the following order form and return it to Seven Locks Press, PO Box 25689, Santa Ana, CA 92799 or call toll-free 800-354-5348.

❏ YES! Send me _____ copies of *American Indian Artifacts* for $18.95 per copy plus a $4.00 shipping and handling charge for the first book and $1.00 for each additional book.

_____
Name

_____
Address

_____
City   State   Zip

Quantity   **Total**

_____ *American Indian Artifacts* - $18.95 $ _____
         Shipping & Handling - $4.00 for first book   _____
                      $1.00 for each add'l book   _____
         Total Enclosed $ _____

Payment Method

❏ Check or money order enclosed (payable to Seven Locks Press)

❏ Visa

❏ Mastercard

_____
Card #   Exp Date

_____
Signature

Other Offerings from Seven Locks Press

Cheyenne Journey   Cloth
Morning Star, Our Guiding Light   0-929765-50-8
by Doreen "Walking Woman" Pond $29.95
and Arthur L. McDonald
Foreword by Senator Ben Nighthorse Campbell

Much more than just history, for the first time centuries-old wisdom is shared with the outside world. *Cheyenne Journey* weaves the story of the Northern Cheyenne people with legends, poems and photographs from the beginning of time through to the present-day success of the Dull Knife Memorial College and Foundation.

National Public Radio   Cloth
The Cast of Characters   0-929765-19-2
by Mary Collins $39.95
Photographs by Jerome Liebling

This visually stunning and engagingly written book traces the history of NPR from its tentative beginnings in 1971, through its financial crisis and growth in the 1980s to its current status as a preeminent source of news and entertainment.

Final Curtain   Paper
Eternal Resting Places of Hundreds of   0-929765-53-2
Stars, Celebrities, Moguls, Misters & Misfits $18.95
by Margaret Burk & Gary Hudson

Ever wonder how the rich and famous, the stars and celebrities of the world, made their exit? *Final Curtain* has all the details. Filled with the secrets and stories that only the true "Hollywood insiders" know— from solved (and unsolved) mysteries to unusual last requests, weird and wonderful epitaphs, and fabulous funerals—this book has it all!

" What a wonderful recall of memories for those of us who were there."

— Bob Hope

To order please contact Seven Locks Press, PO Box 25689, Santa Ana, CA 92799 or call toll-free 800-354-5348.

Printed in the United States
6809